AF531820

MUGHAL POETRY
Its Cultural and Historical Value

MUGHAL POETRY
Its Cultural and Historical Value

HĀDĪ HASAN

AAKAR

MUGHAL POETRY
Its Cultural and Historical Value
Hādī Hasan

First Published, 1951
Reprinted with a new Preface by Mushirul Hasan, 2008

ISBN 978-81-89833-49-7

Published by
AAKAR BOOKS
28 E Pocket IV, Mayur Vihar Phase I, Delhi-110 091
Phone : 011-2279 5505 Telefax : 011-2279 5641
aakarbooks@gmail.com; www.aakarbooks.com

Printed at
Mudrak, 30 A Patparganj, Delhi-110 091

DEDICATED

TO

Ḥājī Muḥammad Naẓīr Ḥusayn of Madras

equally eminent as a thinker, patriot and philanthropist

بخشد دل تو فیض و نجوید سبب چو مهر   جانها همه فداي دل مهربان تو

AND TO

Begum Naẓīr Ḥusayn

'fair as a star when only one is shining in the sky'

یا رب چه گوهري تو که افروخت در ازل   جانهاي قدسیان همه از نور جان تو

CONTENTS

PREFACE

In the 1950s, the Aligarh Muslim University was headed by Dr. Zakir Husain. A patron of learning, he recruited some of the brightest intellectuals of Aligarh. Dr. Hadi Hasan was one of them. Like many in this generation, he did not produce many books, but he was a very well read person with an eclectic bent of mind. He and Dr. Mohammad Habib were the two stalwarts in an institution that had just recovered from the shock of partition. They were both excellent teachers.

This small book on Mughal poetry was published in 1952. It is of great value for outlining the main features of Persian poetry under the Mughals. You may also discover the poetry of the Mughal royalty. A small section deals with the poets who were weighed in silver.

Persian poetry is, in general, rich and scintillating. Given its traditions, it bridges the gulf between man's spiritual quest and his striving in this world.

The Mughals spoke and wrote in the Persian language. Indeed, the reign of Jahangir and Shah Jahan were the high points in the evolution of Persian Poetry. On the many poets, Urfi Shirazi stands out as a poet cast in the classical mould.

I commend this book as an introduction to the vibrant Persian poetry under the Mughals.

10 April, 2008 **Mushirul Hasan**

PREFACE

MUGHAL poetry is the Persian poetry of Mughal India and it is here presented in such fashion that those who do not know Persian may not find the Persian originals obstacles in their way whereas those who know Persian may be able to read the original and the translation simultaneously, for no translation, howsoever exquisite, can take the place of the original : the translation is the picture, but the original is the bride.

The book has been written with the barest economy of words : "ye shall not be heard for your much speaking." Also there is much in it which is new and novel. And if I have done nothing in life, I have at least found the unique *dīwān* of Falakī in Madras, of the Emperor Humāyūn in Patna and of Kāhī in Lucknow. For the loan of the last two *dīwāns* my gratitude to my talented friends Prof. 'Askarī of Patna and Prof. Mas'ūd Ḥasan Riḍwī of Lucknow is in my heart, mind, tongue. Falakī's *dīwān* has already been printed ; Humāyūn's is in press ; and Kāhī's is nearing completion. It is curious how Life moves in a circle. The impetus for all the writing I did in the past came from Dr. Dhākir Ḥusayn, Vice-Chancellor of 'Alīgarh Muslim University ; and the stimulus for all the writing I am now doing also comes from him. I know that he reads with pleasure what I write, though what I write is hardly worth reading, especially by an educationist of his eminence.

To my many friends in Madras—Ḥājī Naẓīr Ḥusayn, Prof. A. W. Bukhārī, Messrs. Ḥājī Jamālu'd-Dīn, 'Abdu'l-'Azīz Khān, M. A. A. Sathār and that man of vision, the founder of a college in Kurnool and the Principal of Presidency College, Dr. 'Abdu'l-Ḥaq—who have always received me with open arms, what shall I say ? "Perishable is every edifice that you see save the edifice of love which is imperishable." Fortunately, Dr. 'Abdu'l-Ḥaq has now been appointed Pro-Vice-Chancellor of 'Alīgarh Muslim University—a just but tardy recognition of his scholarship and dynamic energy.

Finally I thank the printers for printing well what was not easy to print at all. The Director, Janāb Sayyid Aṣghar Ḥusayn and the Asst. Director, Shrī R. Rajagopal have made the Hyderabad Government Central Press one of the best presses in India of to-day and I hope that they and Messrs. Ram Chander and Ja'far will extend to me the same courtesy and co-operation when the *Dīwān-i-Kāhī* goes to press.

HĀDĪ ḤASAN,
'Alīgarh,
30 *April* 1952.

GENERAL CHARACTERISTICS OF MUGHAL POETRY

GENERAL CHARACTERISTICS OF MUGHAL POETRY

THE æsthetic value of Mughal architecture, painting, jewellery, even gardens and music has not been questioned ; but on Mughal poetry, world-opinion is sharply divided. And since the object of these lectures, delivered under the auspices of a trust created for the dissemination of Islamic culture by a noble lady who herself was cultural Islam in her own lifetime, is to show that Mughal poetry is a thing of beauty, more inflammable than Tān Sen's Dīpak Rāga,[1] I shall first of all argue the case on behalf of the dissentients, that is try to explain why, in contrast to the Indians and the Turks, Persians and Europeans are not enamoured of Mughal poetry. There are many aspects of Mughal poetry on which systematic work has not been done, one of them being the Anglo-Persian dislike and the Indo-Turkish fondness for Mughal poetry.

" After Jāmī, " says Gibb in his *History of Ottoman Poetry*,[2] " 'Urfī and Fayḍī were the chief Persian influences on Turkish poetry until they were superseded by Ṣā'ib : the novelty in this style lay, apart from the introduction of a number of fresh terms into the conventional vocabulary of poetry, in the deposition of rhetoric from the chief seat and the enthronement of loftiness of tone and stateliness of language in its stead. " " Ḍiyā Pāshā in that portion of his metrical Introduction to the *Kharābāt* which discusses the Persian poets, after praising Jāmī, proceeds to speak of 'Urfī and Fayḍī as follows :

> Fayḍī and 'Urfī run neck and neck ; they are the leaders of the later time.
> In Fayḍī is eloquence and freshness ; in 'Urfī, sweetness and fluency.
> In Fayḍī are fiery exhortations, while 'Urfī is strong in elegies.
> But if pre-eminence be sought, excellence still remains with Fayḍī :
> Fayḍī is clear throughout ; no dots need be added to his commentary."[3]

The last reference is to Fayḍī's *Sawāṭi'u'l-Ilhām*, a commentary on the *Holy Qur'ān* consisting of undotted letters throughout : for example, all the dots in the two proper names يوسف and فرعون have been eliminated by rendering Joseph as ' the son of the blind ' ولد الاعمى and Pharaoh as ' the enemy of Moses ' عدو موسى . " Such a

1. It is reported that when Tān Sen sang the Dīpak Rāga in the presence of Akbar, the palace caught fire ; and since then notwithstanding the protection afforded by insurance companies and the fire-brigade, this inflammable and combustible Rāga has remained unsung.

2. Vol. I, pp. 5, 127, 129.

3. Prof. E. G. Browne's *Literary History of Persia*, Vol. IV, pp. 242-243.

commentary is an innovation," said the critics—to which Fayḍī replied: "The Islamic formula for the protestation of faith: 'there is no God but God and Muḥammad is the Apostle of God' لا اله الا الله محمد رسول الله also consists of undotted letters throughout."

Regarding this commentary, Riḍā Qulī Khān writes in the *Majma'u'l-Fuṣaḥā* 1295 A.H., "Fayḍī has laboured unnecessarily" [كلفتي بي حاصل كشيده].[1] And the same Persian anthologist says of 'Urfī, d. 999/1590: "I have frequently glanced at the *dīwān* of 'Urfī: the style of his poetry is disliked by the people of Īrān at the present time" [ديوان عرفي مكرر بنظر رسيده - سياق اشعارش پسنديدهٔ اهالي اين عهد نيست]; [2] and of the poet Ṣā'ib, whose date of death by a small oversight has been given by Prof. Browne on the same page, 265 of the 4th volume of his *Literary History of Persia*, as 1080 and 1088 A.H., Riḍā Qulī Khān says: "Though Ṣā'ib's *dīwān* consists of 100,000 verses, he has a strange poetical style which no one appreciates today" [با آنکه صد هزار بيت ديوان دارد درطريق شاعري طرزي غريب داشته که اکنون پسنديده نيست].[3] Similarly, the anthologist Luṭf 'Alī Khān says in his *Ātashkadah*, of Kalīm, Shāh Jahān's poet-laureate d. 1061 A.H.: Kalīm" has every kind of verse; but the verse which is good he does not have":

از هر قسم شعر دارد ليکن شعري که قابل باشد ندارد -

The significant fact about this denunciation of Mughal poetry is that it is a condemnation by the Persians of the Persians themselves, for with the exception of Fayḍī nearly all the notable poets of the Mughal period were Persians, born in Persia who had come to India either reluctantly:

1. "If safe and sound I cross the Sind
   Blacken my face ere I wish for Hind." (Khwājah Kalān)
2. Kāhī, thou art the nightingale of the rose-garden of Kābul: thou art neither a kite nor a raven to go to Hindustān. (Qāsim-i-Kāhī, d. 988 A.H.)

   کاهي تو بلبل چمن آراي کابلي　　زاغ و زغن نهٔ که بهندوستان شوي
3. Where two men can be purchased for a rupee, man is known and the value of man is known. (Ḥaydarī, d. 1002 A.H.)

   جائي که بيک رپيه دو آدم بخرند　　آدم معلوم و قدر آدم معلوم

or cheerfully:

1. The means of acquiring perfection do not exist in Īrān: the henna dye acquires no colour till it comes to India. (Salīm of Ṭihrān, d. 1057/1647)

   نيست در ايران زمين سامان تحصيل کمال　　تا نيآمد سوي هندستان حنا رنگين نشد
2. India may be called a second Paradise for whosoever quits this garden, suffers from remorse. (Kalīm, d. 1061/1651)

   توان بهشت دوم گفتنش باين معني　　که هرکه رفت ازين بوستان پشيمان شد
3. Because of my love for India, my eye is located at the back of my head in such wise that when I set out for Īrān, I do not see what is ahead of me. (Kalīm)

   ز شوق هند زان سان چشم حسرت در قفا دارم　　که رو هم گر بره آرم نمي بينم مقابل را

---

1. Ṭihrān *ed.*, Vol. II, p. 26.　2. *Ibid.*, Vol. II, p. 24.　3. *Ibid.*, Vol. II, p. 24.

4. Like the desire to go to India which possesses every (human) heart, there's not a head which does not dance to the tune of thy love. (Ṣā'ib, d. 1080/1670)

همچوعزم سفر هند که در هر دل هست رقص سوداي تو در هيچ سري نيست که نيست

Bābur rebuked the sentiments of Khwājah Kalān:

"Give a hundred thanks, Bābur, that the generous Pardoner
Hath given thee Sind and Hind and many a kingdom."

but his grandson, Akbar, otherwise ultra-Indian, seems also to have pined and fretted for his Transoxanian home:

My life has all been spent in exile and separation, in grief and sorrow.	عمرم همه در فراق و هجران بگذشت با درد و الم
How useless has been this precious life—spent in pain and affliction!	اين عمر گرانمايه چه ارزان بگذشت در رنج و ستم
The life which in Samarqand and Herāt was one round of joy and pleasure	عمري که بشد صرف سمرقند و هري با عيش و طرب
In Agra, alas! was utterly ruined by worry and anger.	افسوس که در اگره ويران بگذشت با غصه و غم

More severe than the Persians is Mr. Vincent Smith in his stricture on Mughal poetry (*Akbar the Great Moghul*, pp. 415-416, Oxford 1917):

"The versifiers or so-called poets were extremely numerous. Abu'l-Faḍl tells us that although Akbar did not care for them, 'thousands of poets are continually at court and many among them have completed a *dīwān* (collection of artificial odes) or have written a *mathnawī* (composition in rhymed couplets).' The author then proceeds to enumerate and criticize 'the best among them' numbering 59 who had been presented at court. He further names 15 others who had not been presented but had sent encomiums to His Majesty from various places in Persia. Abu'l-Faḍl gives many extracts from the writings of the select 59 which I have read in their English dress without finding a single sentiment worth quoting, although the extracts include passages from the works of his brother, Fayḍī, 'the king of poets' which Abu'l-Faḍl considered to enshrine 'gems of thought.'"

"It is doubtful how far a foreigner is competent to criticize," writes Prof. Browne on the criterion of selection and divergence of foreign from native taste on p. 226 of the 4th volume of his *Literary History of Persia*. "A foreigner may say that he personally admires or dislikes a poet, but I doubt if he should go so far as to class him definitely on this ground as good or bad. The taste of even the Turks and Indians who are more familiar with Persian poetry than we can easily become differs very considerably from that of the Persians who must be reckoned the most competent judges of their own literature."

There can be no doubt, therefore, that Mughal poetry has not appealed to Iranians and Europeans—to those who have read it in the original and to those who have read it in translations. Does the fault lie with Mughal poetry or with the critics or with both ? And if the fault lies with Mughal poetry, why have the critics not explained, analysed and dissected the fault ?

Now a criticism based on translations is of doubtful value. Every precious stone committed to a cunning polisher grows more effulgent by the loss of substance, but a translation of chronograms, puns and antiphonies in which Mughal poetry happens to be particularly rich is not the cutting of a gem but its pulverization. The weight remains but the size and colour of the stone are gone. And even the weight suffers loss when the translation is inaccurate. The third volume of Badā'ūnī's *Mūntakhabu't-Tawārīkh* written during Akbar's lifetime in 1004 A.H. is a mine of information on Mughal poetry and it has been translated into English by an eminent scholar, Sir Wolseley Haig. But can we judge Mughal poetry by Sir Wolseley's translation ? Here is his rendering of one of Marwī's couplets in praise of the Prophet's ascension to Heaven :

> The sweet-voiced nightingale of the garden of revelation
> Whose eyes were anointed with the antimony of us base crows.[1]
> خوش الحان عندليب باغ ابلاغ　　　مكحل نرگسش از كحل ما زاغ

It is a Persian verse and in Persian ما means 'we' and زاغ means 'crows'—whence "us base crows." But ما زاغ here is "did not turn aside"—an Arabic citation from the *Holy Qur'ān*, chapter 53, verse 17: ما زاغ البصر وما طغي *i.e.* "the eye (of the Prophet) did not turn aside nor did it exceed the limit" at the time of his ascension to Heaven. An apposite citation from the *Holy Qur'ān* is misconstrued as Persian, and a flawless diamond has been ground to powder !

So much for the critic who has read Mughal poetry in an English dress. To proceed now to the Persians, "the most competent judges," as Prof. Browne says, "of their own literature."

Persian criticism of Mughal poetry is altogether vague : not a single Persian critic has given the reasons for his dislike of Mughal poetry. In his *Literary History of Persia,* Vol. IV, p. 245, Prof. Browne gives one of these reasons, namely, Mughal disparagement of Iranian heroes. Says 'Urfī (*Shi'ru'l-'Ajam,* Vol. III, p. 88) :

Judge fairly why should Abu'l-Faraj Rūnī and Anwarī not deem death an unexpected advantage ?	بهر چه غنيمت نشارند عدم را	انصاف بده بوالفرج و انوري امروز
In God's name, let them be miraculously restored to life —to pick up my pen when I have cast it away.	تا من قلم اندازم و گيرند قلم را	بسم الله ز اعجاز نفس جان ده شان باز
None can produce my soul-entrancing verses, neither Anwarī nor any other fellow.	نه انوري نه فلاني دهد نه بهاني	تفرجي كه من از بهر روح ساز دهم
Khāqānī wanted the life-giving breath of Jesus—wherefore I am sending these verses to Shirwān by the morning breeze.	بامدادصبااينك‌فرستادم‌بشروانش	دم عيسي تمنا داشت خاقاني كه برخيزد

1. English translation of Badā'ūnī's *Muntakhab* by Sir Wolseley Haig, Vol. III, p. 250, Cal. 1925.

Wherefore did Sa'dī glory in a handful of the earth of Shīrāz, if he did not know that it would be my birthplace and abode ?	نازش‌سعدي بمشت خاک شیراز ازچه بود گرنمیدانست باشد مولد و ماواي من

Invidious comparisons, however, are not confined to persons : they extend to places and monuments held in national esteem :

1. By Qāsim Arslān (Badā'ūnī's *Muntakhab*, text, III, p. 185) who died in 995 A.H. :

The torrents rushing down the slopes of the grand fort (of Ajmere) would carry away a thousand mountains like Alwand and Elburz.	برد سیل آن قلعهٔ پر شکوه هزاران چو الوند و البرز کوه

2. By Mullā Ṭughrā (*Kulliyāt*, Bankipore MS., List No. 677, f. 382[a]) who died in 1078 A.H. :

Two hundred Arches of Ctesiphon do not make a single brick of the city-wallsof Delhi.	دو صد طاق کسري چو گردد فراهم نباشد چو یک خشت دیوار دهلي

Another reason is the obvious fact that though the poets were born in Persia, their poetry was born in India and grew up under the influence of Hindī. This growth was in three different directions. Firstly, new words were coined, *e.g.* شکسته نواز 'the mender of the broken' for اعلیحضرت 'His Majesty' ; جاگیر 'a fief' for مستغل (Qudsī's *Kulliyāt*, Bankipore MS., List No. 684 f. 122[b]) :

He summoned the army-chiefs and sent them to their jāgīrs (fiefs).	سران سپه را ز ره خواند پیش فرستاد شان سوي جاگیر خویش

Secondly, the original meaning of words was distorted : "gharīb" means foreigner : in India, it means a 'destitute :'

On the graves of poor people, like ourselves, there is neither a lamp nor a rose : (here) no moth burns its wings ; no nightingale sings a song.	بر مزار ما غریبان ني چراغي ني گلي ني پر پروانه سوزد ني صداي بلبلي

A Persian, however, would read "on the graves of foreigners like ourselves ;" and obviously fail to appreciate the charm of the verse ascribed by some to the Empress Nūr Jahān and by others to the Princess Zību'n-Nisā.

Thirdly, Hindī words which no Persian can understand, were incorporated in the Mughal poetry of India, for example :

1. By the Emperor Akbar, d. 1014 A.H. (*'Urafātu'l-'Āshiqīn*, Bankipore MS. No. 685, f. 121[a]) : "chūrī" is a bangle. *Notice the play on Manyār and 'man + yār :'*

Because of separation from Miss Manyār my heart is lacerated with grief.	منیار که خون شد دلم از دوري او من یار غمم ز دست مهجوري او

در آئنهٔ چرخ نه قوس قزح است　　عکسیست نمایان شده از چوری او

Seen in the mirror of the sky is not a rainbow but the reflection of her bangle (fallen off from the wrist).

2. Also by Akbar : چیته not یوزپلنگ is the word used for the hunting-leopard and کاله not آهوی سیاه for the antelope :

چیتهٔ پادشاه کاله گرفت　　خون او دشت را چو لاله گرفت

The hunting-leopard of the king has caught the antelope : his blood has made the field a bed of tulips.

3. By Kāhī, d. 988 A.H. :

چیتهٔ[1] شاه که او صید کند آهو را　　همه تن چشم شده تا که ببیند او[2] را

When it attacks the deer, the king's cheetah becomes all eyes.

4. By Qāsim Arslān, d. 995 A.H. :

طالع و بخت همایون بین که هنگام شکار　　باشه و بازت همای و چیته ات ضیغم گرفت

Look at His Majesty's horoscope : at the time of hunting, his falcon seizes the phœnix and his cheetah, the lion.

5. By the Emperor Jahāngīr, d. 1037 A.H. : " the King's cheetah has seized the antelope "—to which a courtier replied, " with blood the field has become a bed of tulips " :

چیتهٔ پادشاه زد کاله　　گشت صحرا ز خون پر از لاله

6. By Ṭālib-i-Āmulī, poet-laureate of Jahāngīr : " rām-rangī," not " bādah " is used for the evening cup of wine :

نئیم منکر صهبا ولیک میگوئیم　　که رام رنگی ما نشهٔ دگر دارد

We are not opposed to the morning draught but we maintain that our evening cup of wine produces an entirely different intoxication.

7. By Abū Ṭālib Kalīm, poet-laureate of Shāh Jahān : " mahājan," not " tājir," is used for a general merchant :[3]

فتاده در دکان یک مهاجن　　همه سرمایهٔ دریا و معدن

In the shop of every general merchant (of Agra) is contained all the produce of the sea and mine.

8. Again by Kalīm :[4]

مه بر وعدهٔ تنبولیان دل　　که جز خون خوردن از وی نیست حاصل

Set not thy heart on the promises of the pān-seller : the outcome thereof is nought but grief.

---

1. In original MS. چته　　2. The او refers to the deer : "that it may see the deer."
3. *Kulliyāt-i-Kalīm*, Hyderabad State Library, MS. No. 1225 f. 73^{a}.
4. *Ibid.*, f. 73b *et seq.* Also *Shi'ru'l-'Ajam*, Vol. III, p. 211.

What shall I say of the clean beauty of the laundry-maid? What shall I say of that unveiled darling?	ز حسن شستهٔ دهوبی چگویم — از آن بي پرده محبوبي چگویم
Silly and pretty is the Pathān girl whose vanity makes life impossible.	غرور حسن با جهل پٹهانی — چو گردد جمع نتوان زندگاني
The fair Rājpūt idols, born to Muslims, have thrown to the winds the patience of lovers.	بتان راجپوت و شیخ زاده — شکیب عاشقان بر باد داده
What a flaming candle without smoke is the Champā flower which sets ablaze a pile of aloeswood!	چه چنپه شعلهٔ شمعي ست بیدود — که آتش میزند در خرمن عود
I have to visualize symmetry, when I describe the Mawlsarī flower.	ز موزونان نظر دریوزه دارم — که وصف مولسري را برنگارم
The Gurhal flower knows no season, for it is ever in bloom like the face of the beloved.	گل گڑهل نه فهمیدست موسم — شگفته چون رخ یار است دایم
The sapling of the Nīm is so fragrant that the heart of the Ṭūbā tree in paradise is rent with envy.	نهال نیمش از بس‌خوش‌نسیم است — دل طوبي ز رشک آن دو نیم‌است

The pān-juice has displaced the lip-stick; the dhobie, the sāqī; the Pathān girl and the Rajput maiden, the fair ones of Khaṭā (Cathay) and Khutan; the Champā and Mawlsarī, the jessamine and the anemone; the Gurhal and the Nīm, the Arghawān and the Chanār. Why blame the Persian if he finds the Indian air a trifle oppressive?

With Mullā Ṭughrā who came to India from Meshed during the beginning of Shāh Jahān's reign and died in Kashmīr in 1078/1667 the Indian air thickens and deepens. Mullā Ṭughrā toured through the whole length and breadth of India from Peshawar to Hyderabad-Deccan, and Gujarat to Bengal and wrote a descriptive praise of all the provinces and the cities he visited, Bengal, Panipat, Tanisar, Delhi, Oudh, Mutthra, Agra, Etawah, Banaras, Orissa, Hyderabad, Ajmere, Gujarat, Tattah, Lahore, Peshawar and Kābul. Says he in his unpublished *Kulliyāt*, Bankipore MS., List No. 677, f. 382[a], *et seq*:

Whosoever drinks the water of Panipat becomes glib-tongued like a parrot.	ز پانی‌پت آنکس که نوشیده پانی — چو طوطي شده سبز رطب اللساني
Two hundred Arches of Ctesiphon do not make a single brick of the city-walls of Delhi.	دو صد طاق کسري چو گردد فراهم — نباشد چو یک خشت دیوار دهلی
The fresh air of Mutthra makes every stone brought from the mountain-side an entrancing idol.	گر از کوه آرند در متره سنگي — شود از هوایش بت شوخ و شنگي

Khiḍr comes to the Agra road to be a guide for the tourist who loves Agra.

خضر میدود ، بر سر راه اگره   که گردد دلیل هوا خواه اگره

And if thou thinkest Khutan is superior to Oudh, thou art mistaken : hold off thy speech.

گر از اوده بهتر شماري ختن را   خطا میکني ، واگذار این سخن را

Every Indian city is one vast treasure-house but let there be no misunderstanding : the poet's praise is mere art for art's sake : he has not been inspired as he himself states in Hindī by considerations of food and drink, give and take :

مرا زین دیاري سراپا خزینه   " نه لینه نه دینه نه کانه نه پینه "

Excellent for home-consumption, can this kind of poetry be expected to circulate in Ṭihrān and Iṣfahān ?

In poets born in India, the Indian element is naturally more pronounced : it reaches its peak in the works of Fayḍī who is among the few Muslim Sanskritists India has produced. He translated Bhāskara's mathematical treatise, the *Līlāvatī* in 995 A.H., the first two parts of the *Mahābhārata* in 997 ; and produced the *Shāriqu'l-Ma'rafat*, the *Kathā Sārit Sāgar* and the mathnawī named *Nal Daman* in 1003 A.H. Here is a fragment reserved for the elite. Commenting on a stiff verse of Adīb-i-Pīshāwarī, 'Abdu'r-Rasūl had said : " Only one man in a thousand can understand this verse. " " I have written the verse for that one man " was Adīb's reply. But to return to the fragment. (India Office MS. of Fayḍī's *dīwān*, No. 3155, f. 289[a]).

حمل آلا و ثور اوبا و جوزا را بود کاچها   ز سرطان است ڈاها وآنگهي بهر اسد ماٹا

دگر از سنبله پاٹها و از میزان بود راتا   بدان صورت که عقرب راست نوجا، قوس را بهادها

پس آنگه جدي کهکه ، دلو گوسا ، حوت را داجها   حکیم هند بست این نقش حکمت با دل دانا

الهي باد تا باشد سپهر و گردش اختر   فروغ کوکب بخت شهنشاه جهان آرا

For the Ram, Ālā ; for the Bull, Ūbā ; for the Twins, Kāchhā ; for the Crab, Ḍāhā ; for the Lion, Māṭā.

For the Virgin, Pāṭhā ; for the Scales, Rātā ; for the Scorpion, Nawjā ; for the Archer, Bhādhā.

For the Goat, Khakha ; for the Bucket, Gawsā ; for the Fish, Dājhā—this wise law has been laid down by the philosophers of India.

Till movement belongs to the spheres and the planets, may the star of His Majesty's good fortune retain its brilliance !

Hindus do not name their children blindly : the auspicious names differ according to the position of the Sun in the Zodiacal Sign at the time of birth. In Aries, the auspicious names are Ālā, *i.e.*, those which begin with Ā and Lā, *A*mar Singh, *Lā*lā Rām ; in Taurus, they should begin with Ūbā, *i.e.*, Ū and Bā, *U*mrao Singh, *Bā*bū Lāl ; in the Gemini, with Kāchhā—Kā and Chhā, *Kāshī* Rām, *Chha*ttar Singh ; in Cancer, with Ḍāhā —Ḍā and Hā, *Dā*l Chand, *Ha*rī Singh ; in Leo, with Māṭā—Mā and Ṭā, *Mā*n Singh, *Ṭā*bar Singh ; in Virgo with Pāṭhā—Pā and Ṭhā, *Pāṭ*ī Rām, *Ṭhā*kur Singh ; in Libra with Rātā—Rā and Tā, *Rā*m Singh, *Tā*rā Chand ; in Scorpio, with Nawjā—Naw and

Jā, *Naw*bat Rām, *Jā*nkī Parshād ; in Sagittarius, with Bhādhā—Bhā and Dhā, *Bhā*ri Chand, *Dha*ni Rām ; in Capricornus, with Khakha—Kha and Kha, *Kha*im Chand, *Kha*mman Singh ; in Aquarius, with Gawsā—Gaw and Sā, *Go*mtī Parshād, *Sā*dhū Parshād ; and in the Pisces, with Dājhā—Dā and Jhā, *Dā*tā Rām, *Jha*mman Singh. How many Indians know this ? And can the outsider know what the householder does not know ?

Nevertheless it is not because of Indian words or names or riddles that Persians have become indifferent to Mughal poetry : the cause lies deeper in the heart of things. Khān Zamān, governor of Jawnpūr, killed as a rebel in 974 A.H., had composed the following verse, Badā'ūnī's *Muntakhab*, text, Vol. III, p. 238 :

باریک چو موئي ست میاني که تو داري   گویا سر آن موست دهاني که تو داري

Slender as a hair is thy waist : thou wouldst say, the end of that hair is thy mouth.

This verse produced a flutter in the dove-cot. " Thy mouth is Khiḍr's fountain of life," said Badā'ūnī, " and thy tongue is a fish in that fount."

سر چشمهٔ خضراست دهاني که تو داري   ماهي ست در آن چشمه زباني که تو داري

Another poet said that the sweetheart's mouth was only an imaginary thing, really incorporeal, to which the sweetheart replied : " Thou art right."

گفتم که گماني ست دهاني که تو داري   گفتا که یقین است گماني که تو داري

The Mughal poet may be right if finding the hair-thin mouth of the sweetheart a bit too thick he reduces it to zero ; but I think the Persian is even more right if finding all this Indian subtlety a bit too thick he also reduces to zero his appreciation of Mughal poetry.

Everyone knows that the sweetheart's face is the full moon and her eyebrows are crescents—but this is not enough for the poet Sulṭān of Saplak. " How can I liken thy eyebrow to the new moon ? " says he, " for I have seen the new moon in every hair of thy eyebrow." (*Muntakhab*, text, Vol. III, p. 238) :

چون کنم تشبیه ابرویت بماه نو که من   هر سر موئي ز ابرویت هلالي دیده ام

In all countries, at all times, the sweetheart's face is bright, irradiating the home with beams of light and saving much lighting fuel on a dark night, for when she unveils, she is a torch, a burning candle or the full moon or even the resplendent sun. But Ulfatī Qilich Khān who became a commander of 5000 under Akbar goes farther. " When she unveils," says he, " the sun appears no more than a moving particle." (*Muntakhab*, text, Vol. III, p. 188) :

تا ز عارض آفتاب من نقاب انداخته   ذره سان خورشید را اندر حجاب انداخته

Hitherto the sweetheart had the monopoly of light and lustre : " the brightness of her cheeks would shame those stars as daylight doth a lamp ; " and she lies not in a dark grave but a lanthorn for " her beauty makes this vault a feasting presence full of light." But the Mughal poet, Khusrawī of Qā'in is a formidable rival to this skin-deep beauty : all skin and bone with love, his shining bones are so surcharged with inner light that they can function as candles to light his tomb. (*Muntakhab*, text, Vol. III, p. 227) :

ز نور عشق باشد خسروي را دل چنان روشن   که شمع مرقد او میتوان کرد استخوانش را

Did I say the lover was skin and bone ? He is really boneless for, borrowing an idea from Amīr Khusraw, " so much has my mournful body melted in thy absence," says Ashkī of Qum, who died in Agra, " that if thou placest a collar about my neck it falls to my feet."[1]

بسکه تن بگداخت بي او زآتش سودا مرا   گر نهي زنجير بر گردن فتد در پا مرا

And again : " my hair hangs dishevelled from my head down to my feet ; my body appears in the midst of it like a single white hair."[2]

موي ژوليده که آيد زسر من تا پا   زان ميان موي سفيد يست تن من پيدا

Lovers weep profusely :

" In one little body
Thou counterfeit'st a bark, a sea, a wind ;
For still thy eyes which I may call the sea
Do ebb and flow with tears ; the bark thy body is
Sailing in this salt flood ; the winds, thy sighs ;
Who raging with thy tears and they with them,
Without a sudden calm, will overset
Thy tempest-toss'd body."[3]

Shakespeare drowns the body's boat in a sea of tears and Juliet's fine weeping performance is lost. Not so the Mughal poet, Ātashī of Qandahār who came to India in the company of Bābur and died in Lahore in 973 A.H. Having shed an ocean of tears, he offers a free cruise to his sweetheart on that lachrymal sea. " Behold, without thee, my tears have gradually become a sea ; come, sit in my eyes as in a boat and make a voyage of that sea."[4]

سرشکم رفته رفته بي تو دريا شد تماشا کن   بيا در کشتي چشمم نشين و سير دريا کن

Also, iṭ has never occurred to any one to examine what remains in the lover himself when he has shed a sea of tears, rivers of blood. This gap in our knowledge is filled by Yādgār Ḥālatī : " from weeping there remains not in my liver," says he, " so much moisture that the bird of thine arrow could wet his bill thereon : "[5]

نماند آنقدر ازگريه آب درجگرم   که مرغ تير تو منقار تر تواند کرد

A bowl of water— کاسهٔ آب —broke in Jahāngīr's hand. " The bowl was delicate and it could not hold its water," said Jahāngīr in an impromptu hemistich :

کاسه نازک بود و آب آرام نتوانست کرد

Thereupon Qāsim Khān, husband of Nūr Jahān's sister, Manīzhah, immediately supplied the antiphony : " seeing my condition, its eye could not restrain its tears : "

ديد حالم را و چشمش ضبط اشک خود نکرد

---

1. Badā'ūnī's *Muntakhab, ed.* Aḥmad 'Alī, Persian text, Vol. III, p. 186, Calcutta, 1869.
2. *Ibid.*, p. 186.
3. *Romeo and Juliet*, Act III, Sc. V.
4. *Muntakhab*, III, p. 180.
5. *Ibid.*, p. 222.

As the Persian language has one word— کاسه —for a bowl of water " کاسهٔ آب " and for the socket of the eye " کاسهٔ چشم, " when the word کاسه is used, the mind thinks both in terms of the bowl and the socket. But in order to appreciate Qāsim Khān's repartee, it is necessary to shut the eye to the eye-socket : the bowl breaking in Jahāngīr's hand and spilling its water is not like a breaking socket but like an eye breaking into tears. The super-subtlety of Qāsim Khān, therefore, demands that the socket of the eye be converted into the eye of the socket, the کاسهٔ چشم into چشم کاسه — otherwise nothing breaks, neither Jahāngīr's bowl, nor Qāsim Khān's tears, nor the hearts of the people of Madras.

Summing up, therefore, the general conclusion, the disparagement of national heroes and monuments, the use of unfamiliar words, the distortion of the meaning of familiar words, the coinage of new words, and above all, the hair-splitting subtlety of the Indian mind which makes the sweetheart's mouth the end of a hair and then literally splits the hair (Sahmī in Badā'ūnī's *Muntakhabu't-Tawārīkh*, text, Vol. III, p. 243) :

> " Her mouth is like the end of the hair in its delicate proportions, but see
> How the sword of her tongue in speech splits the hair ! "
>
> دهان او سر موئي بود از نازکي بنگر   که چون تيغ زبانش مي شگافد درسخن او را

—these have been the factors responsible for Persian apathy or antipathy to Mughal poetry. But there are few emeralds without a flaw ; and even flawless emeralds were produced by Mughal India.

MERITS OF MUGHAL POETRY

MERITS OF MUGHAL POETRY

WHAT Prof. Ethe happily calls the Indian summer of Persian poetry is the century 1555-1658 A.D. intervening between Humāyūn's conquest of India and the dethronement of Shāh Jahān, when poets were men of wit:

'Urfī means 'well-known:' and Fayḍī's father bore the name of Mubārak which means 'auspicious.' So one day 'Urfī called on Fayḍī whom he found playing with a puppy. 'What may the name of this young master be?' said Fayḍī:

اسم مخدوم زاده چیست

'His name,' said Fayḍī, 'is 'Urfī:' 'his name is well-known'—to which 'Urfī promptly replied: 'Mubārak bāshad;' 'perhaps the name is Mubārak: the name is auspicious.'

when kings were critics:

1. By Ḥayratī:

همچو پروانه بشمعي سر و كار است مرا   كه اگر پيش روم بال و پرم ميسوزد

Like the moth, my business is with the candle: if I press forward, I shall sear my wings.

Humāyūn's spontaneous emendation: "I shall press forward, even if I sear my wings:"

ميروم پيش اگر بال و پرم ميسوزد

2. By Fighānī:

مسيحا يار و خضرش رهنما و همعنان يوسف   فغاني آفتاب من بدين اعزاز مي آيد

With Jesus as a friend, Khiḍr as a guide and Joseph riding by his side—in such fashion comes my glorious sun, O Fighānī.

Akbar's spontaneous emendation: "in such fashion comes my glorious horseman, O Fighānī:"

فغاني شهسوار من بدين اعزاز مي آيد

when poets were potentially or actually weighed against silver, when a hundred thousand tankahs were paid for stealing an ode and when the human mind worked in flashes of lightning :

> " The Emperor Humāyūn," writes Badā'ūnī,[1] " was one night in conversation with Bayram Khān who was overcome by drowsiness. ' Ha ! Bayram Khān ! It is to you that I am speaking,' said Humāyūn reprovingly. ' Yes, sire,' replied Bayram, ' I am attentive ; but I have heard that in the service of kings, a watch should be kept over the eyes, and among darvishes a watch should be kept over the heart, and among learned men a watch should be kept over the tongue ; and I was wondering over which I should keep a watch, for Your Majesty is at once a king, a darvish and a learned man.' "

Equally smart was Bayram's reply when he received the following impromptu quatrain from Humāyūn in 955/1548 : " O companion of my dejected heart, well-proportioned in mind and body ; all the time I think of thee. How fares it with thee and dost thou fret for me ? "[2]

اي آنکه انيس خاطر محزوني　　چون طبع اطيف خويشتن موزوني

بي ياد تو نيستم زماني هرگز　　آيا تو بياد من محزون چوني ؟

" O thou who art essentially the Shadow of God and can never be overpraised," replied Bayram, " since thou knowest how in thy absence it fares with me, why dost thou ask me how I fret for thee ? "[3]

اي آنکه بذات سايهٔ بيچوني　　از هر چه ترا وصف کنم افزوني

چون ميداني که بي تو چون ميگذرد　　چون ميپرسي که. در فراقم چوني ؟

And yet this remarkable man equally brilliant in the field and the palace, with his sword and his tongue, whose *dīwān* of Persian and Turkish verses was in every man's hand, found it fit to plagiarize a ghazal of Hāshim Qandahārī, putting the lines into a different arrangement and offering him 60,000 tankahs by way of compensation. " Is this enough ? " asked Bayram. " Sixty is too little," replied the greedy poet, upon which the figure was rounded off to a lakh of tankahs, *i.e.*, Rs. 10,000. Here is that ghazal of which the exordium is Hāshim's :[4]

Who am I ? One who has allowed the reins of his heart to slip from his hands and without the restraining hand of his heart, has fallen off on the road of grief—	من کيستم عنان دل از دست دادهٔ　　وز دست دل براه غم از پا فتادهٔ

---

1. *Muntakhab*, Vol. III, Eng. tr., p. 267.
2. Firishtah, Neval Kishore ed., p. 239.
3. *Ibid.*, p. 239.
4. *Muntakhab* of Badā'ūnī, Vol. II, Eng. tr., p. 36.
   See also *Dīwān-i-Bayram Khān, ed.* Sir E. Denison Ross, Calcutta, 1910, p. 36, where all the seven verses of the ghazal are given.

Who is wandering like a madman in the skirts of the mountains, and without a will of his own is heading off to the desert.	بي اختيار سر به بيابان نهادۀ	ديوانه وار در كمر كوه گشتۀ
Sometimes like a candle burning in the fire of his heart; sometimes like a wick burning in the heart of fire.	گه چون فتيله با دل آتش فتادۀ	گاهي چو شمع ز آتش دل درگرفتۀ
Little or much is more or less unknown to me, Bayram, who hath never uttered the words, 'more or less.'	هرگز نگفته‌ايم كمي يا زيادۀ	بيرم ز فكر اندک و بسيار فارغم

It was altogether an extraordinary period, this period of Humāyūn, Akbar, Jahāngīr and S͟hāh Jahān. "What's in a name?" says Shakespeare. And yet associated with a *pen-name* is the story of an attempted murder; and clustering round mere names are some of the most exquisite verses that exist in literature. I shall, first of all, give the story that nearly brought on the darkness of death; then cite the verses more effulgent than stellar and lunar and solar light.

> "The poet Sulṭān of Saplak," writes the contemporary Badā'ūnī, "had a disposition well attuned to poetry. When he saw K͟hān Zamān (governor of Jawnpūr) who also used Sulṭān as a poetical name and presented to him an ode in his praise, the K͟hān sent him, as a reward for it, a thousand rupees and a robe of honour, together with a request that he would, for his sake, change his poetical name. He sent back the gift and said: 'Sulṭān Muḥammad is my name which was given to me by my father. How can I give it up? Moreover I wrote poetry under this name many years before you did and obtained much fame by it.' K͟hān Zamān replied: 'If you do not give up the name, I will throw you under the feet of an elephant,' and being enraged, he had an elephant brought on the spot. Sulṭān said, 'Ah! Good fortune is mine! I shall attain martyrdom!' After K͟hān Zamān had intimidated and threatened him for a long time, Mawlānā 'Alāu'd-Dīn Lārī, the K͟hān's tutor, suggested that an ode should be selected from the *dīwān* of Mawlānā Jāmī which was at hand, and if Sulṭān of Saplak could answer it extemporaneously he should be pardoned; if not, the K͟hān should do with him as he had proposed. The poet having stood the test, K͟hān Zamān gave him double the original reward and dismissed him with honour."[1]

Can such things be or have we eaten on the insane root that takes the reason prisoner?

Puns, chronograms, satires, original similes and concepts constitute the salient merits of Mug͟hal poetry. I shall present a series of illustrative examples for, as the poet Sa'dī says, "Musk is that which exhales fragrance and not which is labelled 'musk' by the druggist."

---

1. *Muntak͟hab*, Vol. III, Eng. tr., pp. 328-329.

PUNS

1. By Khān Zamān, governor of Jawnpūr †974 who had sent Ghazālī, d. 980, a purse of a thousand rupees, inviting him to court :[1]

چونکه بيقدر بودهٔ آنجا   سر خود را بگير و بيرون آي

Since thou hast not been esteemed at thy proper value (in the Deccan), take heed or rather *take thy head* and come (for the head of Ghazālī is '*ghayn*' and the numerical value of غ is 1000).

2. By Ḥakīm 'Aynu'l-Mulk Dawā'ī of Shīrāz, who was sent as an envoy to Chingiz Khān of Gujarāt in 1564 A.D., as an ambassador to 'Alī 'Ādil Khān of Bījāpūr in 1577, became Ṣadr of Bengal in 1581 and *Dīwān* of Agra in 1585 and died in 1003 A.H./2nd September, 1595. 'Mardum' means 'a gentleman' and also 'a pupil of the eye :'[2]

منه اي طفل اشک ازخانهٔ چشمم قدم بيرون
که ميايند مردم زادها ازخانه کم بيرون

Remain in thy house, my little tear : well-born pupils (*mardum*) seldom stir out of their homes.

3. By Mawlānā Sa'du'd-Dīn Rahā'ī of Khawāf :[3]

زچشم من چو اشک اي نازنين من روان مگذر
زماني مردمی کن اينچنين ازمردمان مگذر

O my darling, desert me not like a tear : be kind and remain in *the pupil of my eye*.

4. By Ṭālib-i-Āmulī, poet-laureate to Jahāngīr from 1028 to 1036 A.H. 'Hazār' means 'a nightingale' and also 'a commander of 1000 :'

بگلزار معني هزار فصيحم   بمنصب چه شد نيستم گر هزاري

I am *hazār* even if I am not *hazār*—æsthetically, if not officially, *i.e.*, I am a nightingale even if I am not a commander of 1000.

5. By Ṭālib-i-Āmulī to I'timādu'd-Dawlah who had appointed him his seal-keeper in 1028 A.H. 'Muhr' means 'a seal;' and 'mihr' means 'love :'[4]

منت بندهٔ داغدار قديمم   بخادم کنون مهر خود ميسپاري

I am thy old and tested servant ; and now thou art entrusting me with thy seal (muhr).

چومهر تودارمچه حاجت به مهرم   مرا مهرداري به از مهرداري

When I have thy love, do I need thy seal ? Better far to have thy *mihr* (*love*) than to have thy *muhr* (*seal*).

6. By Ṭālib-i-Āmulī to Jahāngīr who had asked him to come to court with his beard cut :[5]

بهشت است بزم تو و در بهشت   من ناتراشيده را راه نيست

Thy assembly is paradise ; and an *uncut* fellow has no place therein.

---

1. Badā'ūnī's *Muntakhab*, Vol. III, text, p. 170. 2. *Ibid.*, p. 223. 3. *Ibid.*, p. 234.
4. Shiblī's *Sh'iru'l-'Ajam*, Vol. III, p. 177. 5. *Ibid.*, p. 183.

7. By Abū Ṭālib Kalīm, poet-laureate of S͟hāh Jahān, when the Rohilla leaders Sea (*Daryā*) and Ornament (*Payrā*) were beheaded in 1040 A.H. :

از رفتن دریا سر پیرا هم رفت   گویا سر این ، حباب آن دریا بود

When *Sea* vanished, *Ornament* also lost his head : thou wouldst say the head of Ornament was *a bubble of the Sea* (in both senses).

8. The best puns are those of the Mug͟hal Emperors : I shall give one example here; others will be cited under " Royal Poetry. " ' S͟hāh Jahān ' means ' the king of the world ' ; and with Mumtāz Maḥal by his side, the Emperor S͟hāh Jahān was watching from his palace at Agra the river Jamna leap and foam on the stones below. To pay a tribute to his wife, the Emperor said : " To see the lustre of thy face the river cometh all this way." " And because of His Majesty's awe, the awe of S͟hāh Jahān, it dasheth its head against the stones, " replied Mumtāz Maḥal :

آب از هواي روي تو مي‌آيد از فرسنگها(شاه جهان)   وز هیبت شاه جهان سرمیزند برسنگها(ممتاز محل)

CHRONOGRAMS

Chronograms usually give the year; but it was reserved for Mug͟hal poets to compose chronograms which give the day, the month and the year, without giving the year—for the day and the month give the year. It was also reserved for Mug͟hal poets to give the year by giving the year, *i.e.*, the numerical value of the letters of the year *also* gives the year. Here are the examples :

1. The birth of Bābur in 888 A.H., the sixth of Muḥarram : *the sixth of Muḥarram*—which gives 888 A.H. :

چون در "شش محرم" زاد آن شه مکرم   تاریخ مولدش هم آمد "شش محرم"

Since that august monarch was born on the sixth of Muḥarram, the date of his birth is *the sixth of Muḥarram.*

2. The first battle of Pānīpat fought in 932 A.H. on the morning of Friday, the seventh of Rajab : it *was morning and Friday and the Seventh of Rajab*—which gives 932 A.H. :

وقت و روز و ماه و سال این ظفر   "صبح بود و جمعه و هفت رجب"

The time and day and the month and year of this victory *was morning and Friday and the seventh of Rajab.*

3. Humāyūn's conquest of Champanir in 940 A.H. on the ninth of the month of Ṣafar : *it was the ninth of the month of Ṣafar*—which gives 940 A.H. :

تاریخ ظفر یافتن شاه همایون   دل جست خرد گفت : "نه شهرصفر بود"

The intellect gave the date of King Humāyūn's victory : *it was the ninth of the month of Ṣafar.*

4. The birth of Akbar in 949 A.H. on the night of Sunday, the fifth of Rajab : *the night of Sunday, the fifth of Rajab*—which gives 949 A.H. :

شب و روز و مه و سال میلاد   "شب یکشنبه پنج رجب" است

The night and day and the month and the year of birth is *the night of Sunday, the fifth of Rajab.*

5. The birth of Akbar's twins, Ḥasan and Ḥusayn, which occurred in 972: *which occurred in nine hundred and seventy-two*—which also gives 972. The chronogram is by Kāhī :

Kāhī inquired of the date of their birth ; and the intellect said : *it occurred in nine hundred and seventy-two.*

کاهي سوال کرد ز تاریخ سال شان گفتا خرد " بنهصد و هفتاد و دو شده "

6. The death of Ghazālī in the year 980 : *the year nine hundred and eighty*, which also gives 980. The chronogram is by Fayḍī :

The intellect wrote the chronogram of his death in two ways (*i.e.*, in figure and words): *the year nine hundred and eighty.*

عقل تاریخ وفاتش بدو طور " سنۂ نه صد و هشتاد " نوشت

7. Akbar's conquest of Gujarāt completed in 980 A.H. on the second of Dhi'l-Qa'dah : *the second of Dhi'l-Qa'dah*—which gives 980. The chronogram is by Qāsim Arslān :

Behold the auspicious horoscope and good fortune of King Akbar who conquered the province of Gujarāt in a short time.

طالع و بخت هایون بین که در اندک زمان
کرد فتح کشور گجرات اکبر پادشاه

Since he returned thence to India on *the second of Dhi'l-Qa'dah*, Arslān's chronogram is *the second of Dhi'l-Qa'dah.*

چون از آنجا " دویم ذي القعده " عازم شد بهند
ارسلان تاریخ آن از " دویم ذي القعده " خواه

8. The death of Kāhī in 988 A.H. on the second of the month of Rabī'u'th-Thānī : *the second of the month of Rabī'u'th-Thānī*—which gives 988. The chronogram is by Fayḍī :

They sought the month and year of his death ; and I replied : "*the second of the month of Rabī'u'th-Thānī.*"

تاریخ مه و سال وفاتش جستند گفتم " دویم از ماه ربیع الثاني "

9. The coronation in 1037 A.H. of Shāh Jahān, that is, 'the king of the world': *Shāh Jahān, that is, 'the king of the world'*—which gives 1037. The chronogram is by Mīr Ṣālī :

The pen of Destiny wrote as the year of his coronation : *Shāh Jahān is Shāh-i-jahān* (Shāh Jahān is the king of the world).

کلک قضا سال جلوسش نوشت " شاه جهان باشد شاه جهان "

10. Shāh Jahān's return from Kashmīr for his second coronation on the Peacock Throne. It was in the year of the Hijrah 1043 : *it was in the year of the Hijrah one thousand forty-three*, which also gives 1043. The chronogram is by Sa'īdā-i-Gīlānī :

It was in the year of the Hijrah one thousand forty-three (1043) that he returned to Delhi with royal pomp and a vast army.

" هزار بود و چهل سه بسال از هجرت "
که شد بدهلي با شاهي و سپاه گران

11. The birth in 1044 A.H of Dārā's son, Sulaymān Shukūh : *Sulaymān Shukūh and Sulaymān Shukūh, i.e.*, Sulaymān Shukūh and Solomon in dignity—which gives 1044 : " سلیمان شکوه و سلیمان شکوه "

12. The birth of Awrangzīb, 1027, *Āftāb-i-'ālam tāb* (*world-illuminating sun*), which gives 1027; his coronation, 1067, *Āftāb-i-'ālam tābam* (*my world-illuminating sun*), which gives 1067; his death, 1117, *Āftāb-i-'ālam tāb-i-man* (*world-illuminating sun of mine*), which gives 1117 A.H.

13. Shāh Jahān's conquest of Balkh in 1056 : "*God has given him the two worlds : what is Balkh ?*"—which gives 1056 A.H. The chronogram is by Abū Ṭālib Kalīm :

"ایزد دو جهان داد باو بلخ چه باشد" تاریخ بود فتح شهنشاه جهان را:

God has given him the two worlds : what is Balkh ? (1056) This is the date of His Majesty's conquest.

14. Shāh Jahān's conquest of Balkh in 1056 : "From the *kingdom of Turān* remove the *ruler of Turān* and in his place enthrone the *Second Lord of Conjunction*"— and count. The counting gives 1056. The chronogram is by Naṣīrā'i-i-Shīrāzī :

والی توران بر آر از ملك توران وانگهي ثانی صاحبقران بنشان بجایش کن حساب

From the Kingdom of Tūrān, *i.e.*, from 747, remove the ruler of Tūrān, *i.e.*, remove 704; and in his place enthrone the Second Lord of Conjunction, *i.e.*, add 1013—which gives 1056.

This Mughal chronogram inspired the Persian poet, Sulaymān-i-Ṣabāḥī to write in 1199: "The pen of Ṣabāḥī wrote: '*From the Royal Palace, 'Alī Murād* made his exit and *Ja'far Khān* sat in his place' "—which gives 1199:

نوشت کلک صباحي ز قصر سلطانی علی مراد برون شد نشست جعفرخان

From the Royal Palace, *i.e.*, from 550, 'Alī Murād, *i.e.*, 195, made his exit, *i.e.*, is subtracted ; and Ja'far Khān, *i.e.*, 1004, sat in his place, *i.e.*, is added —which gives 1199.

SATIRES

1. Ousted by Humāyūn from the throne of Kābul, Kāmrān had sought refuge with Islām Shāh who had received him as an unwelcome guest. "The movement of the revolving sphere," said the fallen Prince in an impromptu verse, "has humbled stiff-necked persons and has imposed uncouth fellows over men of culture."

گردش گردون گردان گردنان را گرد کرد بر سر اهل تمیزان ناقصان را مرد کرد

Later when blinded by Humāyūn's order, he said to the Emperor who had called on him: "whatever thou metest out to me deserves my thanks—whether it be the blinding needle or the piercing blade."

بر جانم از تو هرچه رسد جاي منت است گر ناوک جفاست وگر خنجر ستم

2. By the poet Mīr Rubā'ī Fikrī on the physician Sayfu'l-Mulūk, *i.e.*, the sword of kings, so called because he killed more patients than he cured: " A sharp sword is His Worship Sayfu'l-Mulūk. Yesterday Death said when he had come to take the life of a sick man: ' Everywhere I go, he has been called in first.' "[1]

دي اَجل ميگفت بهر بردن جان مريض   هر كجا رفتيم ، پيش از ما علاجي كرده بود

The death in 970 A.H. of Jāmī's grandson whom Sayfu'l-Mulūk unsuccessfully treated is given by the chronogram: Sayfu'l-Ḥukamā killed (him).

سيف الحكما كشت : ٩٧٠

3. By an unknown poet on the physician Jalāl: " The Angel of Death said to God: ' Thy slave is helpless before Jalāl, the physician. Where I kill one, he kills a hundred. Either depose him or assign to me some other employment.' "[2]

ملک الموت از جلال طبيب   شكوهٔ برد دوش پيش خدا
بنده عاجز شدم ز دست طبيب   ميكشم من يكي و او صد تا
يا ورا عزل كن ازين منصب   يا مرا خدمت دگر فرما

Physicians, however, have ever been the target of attack. A fine Persian satire says: " If thou wert to continue as the chief physician for a year more, thou alone wouldst be living and everybody else would be dead and gone." Also, " a physician's job is the best, safest and most lucrative: if thy patient recovers, thou hast cured him; if he dies, man is mortal. "

4. By Mīr Maḥmūd Maḥwī, Akbar's Chief Secretary for 25 years, died at Agra in 979 A.H., on a horse presented to him by the Emperor Humāyūn: " O exalted King, with an army like Jamshīd's, I have a horse, exceedingly lean and weak. When I mount him, at every two or three steps which he takes, he falls saying: ' Now you carry me for two or three steps.' "[3]

اي خسرو جم سپاه عالي مقدار   دارم اسپي كه هست بس لاغر و زار
بر وي چو شوم سوار در هر دو سه گام   افتد ، كه تو هم-يک دو سه گامي بردار

Similarly, an unknown poet says of a horse: " He goes one or two steps and then says: ' Now do you carry me for an hour or so.' " And Ṭālib-i-Kalīm says: " Because it is always perspiring, that old horse presented by His Majesty is like a boat sailing in water, or rather at anchor."[4]

هميشه ازعرق خويش كشتي است درآب   شده بيكجا از لنگر ركاب مقيم

For the sake of comparison, here are two satires on horses by the poets of Īrān. Anwarī was presented with such an old horse that it died on the very night of its arrival. On the morrow the poet came to court walking on foot. "Surely we presented you with a horse," said the King. "Yes, sire," replied the poet, " but that horse was so swift of foot that in one night he traversed the distance from the earth to heaven."

آنچنان تيز بود در رفتار   كه شباشب بآخرت برسيد

---

1. Badā'ūnī's *Muntakhab*, text, Vol. III, p. 254. 2. *Ibid.*, p. 227. 3. *Ibid.*, p. 322.
4. *Dīwān-i-Abū Ṭālib Kalīm*, Hyderabad State Library MS., No. 1225, f. 57b.

" Surely we presented you with a horse, " said the King to the poet Salmān-i-Sāwajī who had come to court walking on foot. " Yes, sire," replied the poet, " but that horse is at least thirty years senior to me in age and it is disrespectful to sit upon one's elders."

از بنده مهتر است بسي سال راستي　　　گستاخي است بر زبر مهتران نشست

5. By Shaydā on Jahāngīr's poet-laureate, Ṭālib-i-Āmulī. Ṭālib means " desirer "; and the Prophet had said: " The world is a carcase ; the desirers thereof are dogs" الدنيا جيفة وطالبها كلاب . So says Shaydā : " Night and day, my patron, Desirer—(Ṭālib)—runs after the carcase of the world. Has he forgotten the Prophet's tradition : ' The world is a carcase and the *desirer* (ṭālib) thereof is a dog ? ' "[1]

شب و روز مخدومنا طالبا　　　پي جيفهٔ دنيوي در تگ است
مگر قول پيغمبرش ياد نيست　　　که دنياست مردار طالب سگ است

6. In 1047 A.H., Mullā Shaydā composed the following satire on the poet Mīr of Hamadān whose pen-name was ' Divine '—Ilāhī :[2]

O my Mīr who has adopted the pen-name of Divine—Ilāhī—it is improper for a man of silt to style himself " divine."

See how the moist and dry stuff in thy verses has made me reject all works—*divine or Divine's.*

اي مير من که کرده الهي تخلصي　　　از مرد لاي ارچه الهی شدن خطاست
زين رطب و يابسي که بود در کلام تو　　　گر منکر کلام الهی شوم رواست

ORIGINALITY OF CONCEPT

The poets of the Mughal court were not bereft of ideas and though not more than ten per cent. of Mughal poetry has survived, it is possible to gather from that mine, gems of thought more lustrous than the pearls in the rosary of Shāh Jahān.

1. By Qāsim Khān Mawjī of Badakhshān,[3] died 979 A.H.:

Her two nipples of incomparable beauty are as bubbles on the surface of milk.

دو پستانش که در خوبي ست يکتا　　　حبابي گشته از شير آشکارا

2. By Ghazālī of Meshed, died 980 A.H.:

My mind is a pearl-laden sea ; my tongue is a tempered blade.

[4] بحر يست ضمير من که گوهر دارد　　　تيغي ست زبان من که جوهر دارد

The scratch of my pen is the blare of Resurrection : a bird of heaven am I soaring on the wings of eloquence.

صور قلمم نفخهٔ محشر دارد　　　مرغ ملکوتم سخنم پر دارد

1. Shiblī, *Sh'iru'l-'Ajam*, Vol. III, p. 182.　　2. *'Amal-i-Ṣāliḥ*, Vol. III, p. 405.
3. Badā'ūnī's *Muntakhabu't-Tawārīkh*, Calcutta *ed.*, text, Vol III, p. 325.　　4. *Ibid.*, p. 172.

O Ghazālī, I avoid the friend who speaks well of the evil I do.	ای غزالی گریزم از باری	که اگر بدکنم نکو گوید
I prefer the plain blunt fellow who, like a mirror, reveals my faults to my face.	من و آن ساده دل که عیب مرا	همچو آئینه رو برو گوید

3. By Ḥaydarī,[2] died 1002 A.H.:

To leave this perfect world with imperfections on thy head is like emerging unclean from a bath.	که ناقص رفتن از عالم چنان است	که بیرون رفتن از حمام ناپاک

4. By 'Aynu'l-Mulk Dawā'ī,[3] died 1003 A.H.:

This tear of mine will not be restrained, like the child who has learnt to run.	در کنارم ننشیند هرگز	طفل اشکم که دویدن دانست
O Dawā'ī, the desire of union with the fair is an attempt to unite flame and cotton (which kiss as they consume).	اي دوائي طلب وصل بتان	شعله و پنبه بهم دوختن است

5. By Sāqī of Meshed:[4]

From my soul as I weep arises a sigh of grief, even as smoke arises when water is thrown on fire.	زجانم گاه گریه آه دردآلود میخیزد	بلي چون آب برآتش فشاني دود میخیزد
When she passes by me quickly, the tears flow from my eyes: aye tears flow from the eyes dazzled by the sun.	چوتیز بگذرد ازمن، زدیده آب برآید	زدیده آب ز تیزي آفتاب برآید

6. By Naẓmī of Tabrīz:[5]

I saw the fairy-faced Parī Khānum in the bath: I saw a spark of fire sitting in water.	بحامي پري خانم پري رخسارهٔ دیدم	نشسته درمیان آب آتش پارهٔ دیدم

7. By Ghayratī of Shīrāz:[6]

She has shed my blood without shedding my blood— slain me by the dagger of her eye.	هلاک خنجر آن قاتلم که خون مرا	چنان بریخت که یک قطره برزمین نه چکید

8. By Ṭālib-i-Āmulī, poet-laureate of Jahāngīr:

How insipid is life! Thou wouldst say the world was the mouth of a patient.	مزهٔ در جهان نمي بینم	دهر گوئي دهان بیمار است
So completely have I sealed my lips against speech that thou wouldst say the mouth was a wound which has healed.	لب از گفتن چنان بستم که گوئي	دهن برچهره زخمي بود به شد

1. *Kulliyāt-i-Ghazālī*, Br. Mus. MS. Add 25023, f. 411b.
2. Badā'ūnī's *Muntakhabu't-Tawārīkh*, Calcutta *ed.*, text, Vol. III, p. 219.
3. *Ibid.*, pp. 231-232.
4. *Ibid.*, p. 246.
5. *Ibid.*, p. 378.
6. *Ibid.*, p. 292.

اي كاش گوش رغبتم احول بدي چوچشم — تا هرچه گفتي از تو مكرر شنودمي

Would that the ear had a squint like the eye so that whatever thou sayest I could hear once more.

مردم ز رشک چند ببينم كه جام مي — لب بر لبت گذارد و قالب تهي كند

I am dying of envy. How long shall I see the cup of wine place its lips on thy lips and pour out its heart?

گه بدل جلوه كند پرتو او گاه بچشم — قسمت اين شد كه در آئينه و آبش بينم

Behold His lustre reflected from a *mirror* and a *pool*—from my *heart* and my *eyes*!

دشنام خلق را ندهم جز دعا جواب — ابرم كه تلخ گيرم و شيرين عوض دهم

To the evil words I hear I reply with blessings, like a cloud which takes up salt water and gives the sweet.

9. By Ṣā'ib:

دور دستان را باحسان ياد كردن همت است
ورنه هر نخلي بپاي خود ثمر مي افگند

To confer favours on people who are far away is real generosity, for every tree drops fruit at its own feet.

در هيچ پرده نيست ، نباشد نواي تو — عالم پراست از تو و خاليست جاي تو

There is not a note but it hums with thy lays: the world is full of thee; only thy place is empty.

10. By Qudsī:

بزير سبزه ره در كوه و صحرا — چو از عقد زمرد رشته پيدا

Like the thread of an emerald-necklace is the path winding in the green-clad hills and dales.

روز قيامت هركسي در دست دارد نامهٔ
من نيز حاضر ميشوم تصوير جانان در بغل

On the day of judgment every one shall come with his record in his hand: I shall also be there with my sweetheart's portrait tucked under my arms.

قدسي ندانم چون شود سوداي بازار جزا
او نقد آمرزش بكف من جنس عصيان در بغل

Qudsī, how shall the bargain be struck? He, with the cash of forgiveness in His hand; I, with my load of sins tucked under my arms.

11. By Abū Ṭālib Kalīm, poet-laureate of Shāh Jahān:

ما ز آغاز و ز انجام جهان بيخبريم — اول و آخر اين كهنه كتاب افتاداست

We have no knowledge of the beginning and end of the world: the first and last (pages) of this ancient book have fallen out.

وضع زمانه قابل ديدن دو باره نيست — روپس نكرد هركه ازين خاكدان گذشت

The way of the world is not worth seeing a second time: not a man looked back when he left this heap of dust.

If walking without eyes is impossible, how, when we have closed our eyes to the world, do we walk out of it ?	چشم ازجهان چوبستي ازوميتوان گذشت	بی دیده راه اگر نتوان رفت پس چرا
What is this difference in writing, if the hand of the same scribe has written all our scrolls of destiny ?	سرنوشت همه گر از قلم تقدير است	اينقدر فرق ميان خط يک کاتب چيست
Thanks to the king, so sound is his sleep that the watchman needs a watchman.	كه بايد پاسباني پاسبان را	بعهدش آنچنان در خواب امن است
Were everyone to receive his due share of merit, the pearl would acquire all the water of the ocean.	بايستي آب بحر نصيب گهر شود	هر کس اگر بقدر هنر بهره يافتي
Since my eyelashes became tearless, they have fallen in my esteem : who cares for the thread devoid of its pearls ?	اکنون چه کنم رشته که وقتي گهري داشت	تا شد مژه بي اشک فتاد از نظر من
The prohibitionist drinks to your eyes, for *they* have ruined the taverns.	هر کجا ميکدهٔ هست خراب افتاد است	شکر چشم تو کند محتسب شهر کزو
I am dying of grief in the very midst of redressers of grief, like a ship burning at sea.	چون آن کشتي که در دريا بسوزد	ميان غم گساران سوزم از غم
Thou comest soon and yet thou comest late : shouldst thou come sooner than soon what would happen ?	از زود اگر زود تر آئي چه شود	زود آمدنت نظر بشوقم دير است

God is One but His unity embraces opposites : He is the First and the Last, the Manifest and the Hidden : هو الاول هو الآخر هو الظاهر هو الباطن . Consequently, even as Divine perfection is equipoise, any nature, the more excellent it is, the better will it be poised till it reaches Prophethood, the height of creature development. Thus it is that the soul feels an essential affection for equipoise, and a pure proportion, wherever observed, is the means of attracting and agitating the spirit. This principle, if prevailing in the particles of elements, is equipoise of temperament, in music is harmony, in gestures grace, in language eloquence, in body beauty, in mind equity. " Thy equity, O king, makes thee a balance, " says the Persian poet, Rūdakī :

جز برتري نداني گوئي که آتشي   جز راستي نجوئي گوئي ترازوئي

> Thou knowest nought but ascent, art thou a flame ? Thou seekest nought but equity, art thou a balance ?

wherefore, when the king is weighed, he becomes a balance within a balance, for in the words of the Mughal poet, Miān Mīr :

چيزي كه برابري تواند كردن   در پلۀ ميزان تو عدل تو بود

What can balance thee is (only) thy double put in the opposite pan.

The reference is to the weighing ceremony of Shāh Jahān who, like his father and grandfather, used to be weighed against silver, gold and gems on his birthday and New Year's Day and the money was later on distributed in charity. Says Abū Ṭālib Kalīm, the poet-laureate :[1]

The balance which has attained equipoise with His Majesty's weight will hardly lower its beam even for the two worlds.	عجب اگر بدو دنيا دگر فرود آيد سر ترازو كز وزن شاه سامان يافت
With the good fortune which the balance has attained, it would befit the Sun if it were to change its mansion of exaltation (from the Leo to Libra).	سزد كه برج شرف را بدل كند خورشيد ازين سعادت كز وزن شاه ميزان يافت
Until, in the balance of actions, the counterpoise of virtue can never be vice,	هميشه تا نبود در ترازوي اعمال متاع طاعت و عصيان بوزن يكسان يافت
May, in public esteem, thy enemy's scale continue to mount with the weight of his sins!	خفيف باد بميزان ديدها خصمت بدان مثابه كه نتوان سبكتر از آن يافت

These verses need no praise : to gild refined gold, to paint the lily, to throw a perfume on the violet, to add another hue unto the rainbow, to praise praise which has been literally balanced, is wasteful and ridiculous excess.

1. *Kulliyāt-i-Abū Ṭālib Kalīm*, Hyderabad State Library MS., No. 1225, f. 4b-5a.

COURT-POETS OF THE GREAT MUGHALS

COURT-POETS OF THE GREAT MUGHALS

THE poet-laureates of the Great Mughals were only four : Ghazālī *c.* 974-980 A.H. and Fayḍī 988-1004 A.H. under Akbar, Ṭālib-i-Āmulī 1028-1036 under Jahāngīr and Abū Ṭālib Kalīm *c.* 1037-1061 under Shāh Jahān. Awrangzīb had no poet-laureates for he was averse to poetry and the fine arts : he abolished music and dismissed the singers who wailed loud and long before the jharok'ha. " Music is dead and we are going to the graveyard to bury it." " Very well, " said the Emperor, " make the grave deep so that neither voice nor echo may issue from it."

On the other hand, in the words of Abu'l-Faḍl, " thousands of poets were continually at the court of Akbar. " At least fifty of them according to the cumulative evidence of the *Ā'īn*, the *Ṭabaqāt* and the *Muntakhab* (which last work deals with 167 poets of Akbar's time), had produced *dīwāns*, namely : Amānī, Ashkī, Chishtī, Dawrī, Ghaznawī, Judā'ī, Ḥālatī, Ḥalwā'ī, Hijrī, 'Itābī, 'Ishqī, Kāshifī, Khanjar Beg, Maylī, Mullā Maqṣūd, Maẓharī, Nāmī, Naẓmī, Nuwaydī, Payrawī, Ṣarfī, Sipihrī, Tashbīhī, Ḥayratī d. 961 A.H., Saqqā d. 962, Ghurbatī d. 966, Bayram Khān d. 968, Waṣlī d. 977, Marwī d. *c.* 979, Ghazālī d. 980, Rawghanī d. 980, Imāmī d. 981, Rahā'ī d. after 983, Kāhī d. 988, Thānī Khān d. 990, Shīrī d. 994, Mushfiqī d. 994, Nūru'd-Dīn Tar Khān d. 994, Qāsim-i-Arslān d. 995, Thanā'ī d. 996, 'Urfī d. 999, Ḥaydarī d. 1002, Fayḍī d. 1004, Anīsī d. 1014, Naw'ī d. 1019, Sanjar d. 1021, Naẓīrī d. 1021, Ẓuhūrī d. 1024, Malik-i-Qummī d. 1024, Ḥayātī d. after 1024 and Muḥammad Sharīf d. 1030. Even to-day 16 of these *dīwāns* exist in the India Office Library, namely of Ḥayratī, Saqqā, Rahā'ī, Hijrī, Kāshifī, Mushfiqī, Thanā'ī, 'Urfī, Fayḍī, Naw'ī, Sanjar, Naẓīrī, Waṣlī, Malik-i-Qummī, Ẓuhūrī and Muḥammad Sharīf. To this list additions can be made—for example, by the *dīwāns* of Bayram Khān (ed. Sir E.D. Ross, Calcutta), Ghazālī (British Museum), Qāsim Arslān (Bankipore State Library) and Qāsim-i-Kāhī (Lucknow). Unfortunately, however, not more than half a dozen of these *dīwāns* have been published but the greatest tragedy is that the very eyes of Mughal poetry, the *dīwān* of Marwī and the works of Sa'īdā-i-Gīlānī, the artist of the Peacock Throne, are lost.

However to Badā'ūnī's list have to be added the poets of the pre-Akbar and the post-Akbar period. Of these latter, excluding the above-mentioned Sa'īdā, the most important are Ṭālib-i-Āmulī, Abū Ṭālib Kalīm and Hājī Muḥammad Jān-i-Qudsī whose works, together with the rare *dīwān* of Qāsim Arslān, I have examined in MS. form in the Bankipore Library. Rotographs of the unique works of Ghazālī were obtained from the British Museum but the sensational find was the discovery in the house of Prof. Mas'ūd Ḥasan of Lucknow, of the world's solitary copy of the *Dīwān-i-Kāhī*.

PRESENTATION OF POETS AT COURT

When Akbar took his seat on the throne, the audience performed the *kurnish* and then remained standing at their places according to their rank with their arms crossed. The place before the throne remained free : one wing was generally occupied by the grandees of the court and the chief functionaries; on the other wing stood the Qurra, the Mullās and the 'Ulamā.[1] The Mughal Emperors were very punctilious in matters of etiquette. When the poet Niyāzī was presented to Humāyūn, he stepped towards him at the levee with his left foot, whereupon the Emperor remarked that the Mullā was left-handed and commanded him to be led out again and again brought forward.[2] The poet Sulṭān of Saplak, who was for some time Akbar's teacher, placed himself at a darbār before the Khān-i-A'ẓam. When the Mīr Tuzak told him to go back, 'why should not a learned man stand in front of fools ?' said he, and left the hall and never came back.[3] The poet 'Ālim of Kābul, seeing that Abu'l-Faḍl, Qāḍī Khān and others from being Mullās had risen to the rank of Amīrs, petitioned to be admitted as a soldier; but the granting of the petition only made the poet a private, not a military commander (manṣabdār). "By which manṣabdār shall I stand and from what place shall I make my obeisance ?" asked the ambitious poet coming to the darbār from one side. "From where you are now standing," said Akbar, penetrating his design.[4] When the poet Qarārī of Gīlān, brother of Ḥakīm Abu'l-Fatḥ, first came to court as a manṣabdār, he provoked much mirth and laughter for he did not know how to put on his sword. "Soldiering does not suit men like me," he replied; and told the story of Akbar's ancestor, Tamerlane, who, in one of his battles, drew up his army in a certain position, and ordered that the laden camels and the footmen and all beasts of burden should take up a position of safety behind the troops, and that the ladies should remain in the rear of the army. At that moment, the learned men asked where their place should be; and Tamerlane replied, "Behind the ladies !" When the story was reported to Akbar as a rare piece of wit on the part of Qarārī, he ordered that he should be sent to Bengal.[5]

The poet Nāmī d. 1015 A.H., who eventually reached under Akbar the command of a thousand and was sent as ambassador to Persia in 1012 describes "the base degrees by which he did ascend." "When I arrived at court," says he, "I tasted the sticks of the ushers and mace-bearers who keep order and had to endure insults ; and when after a long period of expectation His Majesty bestowed on me a command of twenty men I lost all my buoyancy and bowed my head in acquiescence." "I am not dejected that things have become ill, not well for me. "'Will be,' 'Will be,' will never be: say, 'Be not' and see what will be."[6]

نیم ملول که کارم نکو نشد بد شد　　شود شود نشود گو مشو چه خواهد شد

1. *Ā'īn*, I, p. 160, Blochmann.
2. Badā'ūnī's *Muntakhabu't-Tawārīkh*, tr. Sir Wolseley Haig, Vol. III, pp. 496-497.
3. Rashīdu'd-Dīn Waṭwāṭ says : "Thy darbār is like the sea ; wherefore, the weeds float at the surface and the pearls are at the bottom of the sea."

بحر است مجلس تو و در بحر بیخلاف　　لولو بزیر باشد و خاشاک بر زبر

4. Badā'ūnī, III, p. 375.
5. *Ibid.*, p. 433.
6. Badā'ūnī, English tr., Vol. III, p. 365.

DUTIES OF COURT-POETS

The duties of the court-poet are nowhere defined but they can be gleaned from the *dīwāns* of court-poets. Qāsim-i-Kāhī wrote an ode on the astrolabe because of Humāyūn's interest in astronomy ; and Ghazālī-i-Meshedī wrote a poem in which the elephant and the hunting-leopard occur in every hemistich, because of Akbar's fondness for elephants and cheetahs. " There are 101 elephants selected for the use of His Majesty ;[1] and 1000 leopards are kept in the royal park," [2] writes Abu'l-Faḍl.

Kāhī records the birth of the twins, Ḥasan and Ḥusayn born to Akbar—an event which occurred in 972 A.H. in the chronogram : " *it occurred in nine hundred and seventy-two* :"

Kāhī inquired of the date of their birth ; and the intellect replied : " *it occurred in nine hundred and seventy-two.*"	گفتا خرد "بنهصد و هفتاد و دو شده"	کاهي سوال کرد ز تاریخ سال شان

and Khwājah Ḥusayn-i-Marwī gives 963 and 977 A.H., the dates of Akbar's coronation and Jahāngīr's birth respectively in an ode which consists of chronograms throughout, the first hemistichs giving the first, and the second hemistichs, the second date :

One by one, the verses of Marwī are so faultless (963) that in each couplet you will attain your objective twice (977).	هریکي جوئي ز وي مقصودي در یابي دو بار	یک بیک ابیات مروي بسکه بي عیب آمده
The first hemistich thereof is the date of the King's accession (963) ; from the second, obtain the (date of) birth of the darling of the world (977).	از دویم مولود نور دیدهٔعالم برآر	مصرع اول ز وي سال جلوس پادشاه

He has also produced eight verses whereof the first hemistich gives 977 and the second hemistich 978, the dates of the birth of Jahāngīr and Murād respectively:[3]

	978	**977**
The heavens have given two sons to the King (977) : the faces of both of them are better than the sun (978).	چهرهٔ آن هر دو به از آفتاب	داد دو شهزاده بشاه این سپهر
Hail ! The birth of the heir-apparent is contained in the first hemistich (977)—so says each couplet (978).	گفته ازو مصرع اولی جواب	مژده که مولود شه از اولست
And from the second hemistich of these couplets (977), deduce the (date of) birth of the second prince (978).	مولد شهزادهٔ ثاني بیاب	از دومین مصرع ابیات هم

How the sense of these chaste verses agrees with their numerical value ! Alas for the lost *dīwān* of Marwī !

1. *Ā'īn*, Vol. I, p. 130.
2. *Ibid.*, p. 288.
3. *Muntakhab*, text, Vol. II, p. 133.

Court-poets were essentially court-historians: Qāsim Arslān, for example. records the dates of Akbar's conquest of Gujarāt, 980 A.H.:[1]

Behold the auspicious horoscope and good fortune of Akbar Bād<u>sh</u>āh, who, in a short time, conquered the province of Gujarāt.	طالع و بخت هایون بین که در اندک زمان کرد فتح کشور گجرات اکبر بادشاه
Since he returned thence to India on the second of <u>Dh</u>i'l-Qa'dah, *the second of <u>Dh</u>i'l-Qa'dah*, Arslān, is the date (of conquest).	چون از آنجا دویم ذي القعده عازم شد بهند ارسلان تاریخ آن از "دویم ذی القعده" خواه

and of Bengal, 982 A.H.:[2]

That King, with the pomp of Jam<u>sh</u>īd, arrived in Bengal; and the chronogram of conquest is: "*Akbar <u>Sh</u>āh came to Bengal attended a hundred times by good fortune.*"	رسید آن خسرو جم جاه شد تاریخ اجلالش بصد اقبال اکبر شاه آمد سوي بنگاله

Sa'īdā-i-Gīlānī, known most appropriately as the nonpareil—Bībadal <u>Kh</u>ān—whose verses exist only in fragments preserved in the *Tuzuk-i-Jahāngīrī*, the *Pād<u>sh</u>āh-Nāmah* and the *<u>Sh</u>āh Jahān Nāmah*, supplies interesting minutiæ on the reigns of Jahāngīr and <u>Sh</u>āh Jahān, for example, (*i*) the conquest of the Kāngra Fort in 1029, (*ii*) the fall of a meteorite in 1030 from which a dagger, a knife and two swords were made for Jahāngīr, (*iii*) the construction of a mosque inside the Kāngra Fort in 1031, (*iv*) the death of Mumtāz Maḥal in 1040, and (*v*) the coronation of <u>Sh</u>āh Jahān on the Peacock Throne in 1044 A.H. I shall re-quote the verses which an Emperor deemed it an honour to quote:[4]

I

The Emperor of the world, King Jahāngīr, son of Akbar the King, who, by the decree of Fate, has become King of the Seven Climes.	شهنشاه زمان شاه جهانگیر ابن اکبر شاه که شد بر هفت کشور بادشاه از حکم تقدیري
World-taker (Jahāngīr), world-bestower, world-possessor and world-monarch through whose youthful luck the old world has acquired safety.	جهانگیر[3] و جهان‌بخش و جهان‌دار و جهان‌دارا که از بخت جوان او جهان ایمن شد از پیري
With his conquering sword, he took the Fort and a mental flash supplied the date: "*Jahāngīr's good fortune took this fort*"—1029.	بشمشیر غزا این قلعه را بکشود ـ تاریخش خرد گفتا: "کشود این قلعه اقبال جهانگیري"

1. *Dīwān-i-Qāsim Arslān*, Bankipore MS., No. 249, f. 51a.
2. *Ibid.*
3. Notice the pun on the Emperor's name.
4. All of them are taken from the *Tuzuk-i-Jahāngīrī*, Neval Kishore edition, p. 349 and p. 335.

II

By King Jahāngīr, the world obtained order : raw iron in the form of a meteorite fell in his reign.

!زشاه جهانگیر جهان یافت نظام   افتاده بعهد او ز برق ، آهن خام

With that iron, by his peremptory order, a dagger, a knife and two swords were made.

ز آن آهن شد بحکم عالم گیرش   یک خنجر و کارد با دو شمشیر تمام

III

Nūru'd-Dīn Jahāngīr, son of Akbar the King, is a monarch who has no equal in the world.

نور دین شاه جهانگیر بن اکبرشاه   بادشاهيست که در دهر ندارد ثاني

The cloud of his sword, whereof a drop can raise a flood, took the Kāngra Fort with the aid of God.

قلعهٔ کانگره بگرفت بتائید اله   ابر تیغش که کند قطرهٔ او طوفاني

This mosque, radiant with light, where the foreheads of worshippers beam with lustre, was built by his order.

شد چو از حکم وي این مسجد پرنور بنا   که منور شود از سجدهٔ او پیشاني

And an invisible voice gave the date of construction : " *The mosque of King Jahāngīr is luminous* "—1031.

هاتف از غیب بگفت از پي تاریخ بناش   **مسجد شاه جهانگیر بود نورانی**

IV[1]

When Mumtāz Maḥal left this world, fairies opened in her face the door of paradise.

زین جهان رفت چو ممتاز محل   در جنت برخش حور کشاد

And angels composed the chronogram : " *May Paradise be the abode of Mumtāz Maḥal !*"—1040.

بهر تاریخ ملائک گفتند   **جاي ممتاز محل جنت باد**

Palace news, in chronograms cut like the inner screen of the Tāj, are also a noticeable feature of the poetry of Abū Ṭālib Kalīm who records the birth and coronation of Shāh Jahān, the births and marriages of his four sons, Dārā Shukūh, Shāh Shujā', Awrangzīb and Murād, the defeat of the Uzbeks in 1038, the completion of the palace inside the Agra Fort in 1048 and the conquest of Balkh in 1056. Exigencies of time and space will only permit the citation of some of these chronograms in their barest form :

1. Shāh Jahān's birth, 1000 A.H., " the king of the kings of the world, the qiblah of the universe : "

شاه شاهان جهان قبلهٔ عالم

---

1. *Pādshāh Nāmah* of 'Abdu'l-Ḥamīd Lahori, Vol. I, p. 389.

2. Dārā's birth, 1024, " the first rose of the royal garden : "

گل اولین گلستان شاهي

3. Awrangzīb's birth, 1027, " the world-illuminating sun : "

آفتاب عالم تاب

4. The defeat of the Uzbeks, 1038, " the conquering army : "

لشکر فتح[1]

5. Dārā's marriage with the daughter of Prince Parwīz, 1042 : " the two auspicious stars of the mansion of glory have united : "

قران کرده سعدین برج جلال[2]

6. Shāh Shujā''s marriage with the daughter of Rustam Mīrzā, 1042, " the litter of Bilqīs has come to Jamshīd, its journey's end : "

مهد بلقیس بسر منزل جمشید آمد[3]

7. The completion of the Agra Palace, 1048, " the residence of the high-placed Emperor : " سراي شهنشاه والا محل ; and again, " the palace of good fortune and the place of good luck : " قصر اقبال و محل دولت

The Persian dread of the sea :[4] " the wise man will avoid the boat and the sea : he will not walk to his own grave or allow himself to be nailed alive in a coffin : " *Kulliyāt-i-Ghazālī*, Br. Mus. MS. Add 25,023, f. 411^b :

کي رود عاقل سوي کشتي و بحر　　هرکه شد دیوانه و مبهوت رفت

هیچ دانا شد بپاي خود بگور ؟　　هیچ عاقل زنده در تابوت رفت ؟

Akbar's skill in riding elephants :[5] " the elephant-overthrowing king is Jalālu'd-Dīn Muḥammad Akbar who bestows elephant-loads of silver on his poets " (Kāhī) :

شاه فیل‌افگن جلال الدین محمد اکبر است　　آنکه بخشد فیل زرین شاعران خویش را

Nūr Jahān's skill in shooting tigers :[6] " Nūr Jahān is the tiger-slaying lady, is the Tiger-Slayer's lady, *i.e.*, wife or widow of Shīr Afgan : "

نورجهان گرچه بصورت زن است　　درصف مردان زن شیر افگن است

Shāh Jahān's cruise in a boat : " who ever saw the sun in a boat ? " (Qudsī) :[7]

بغیر از شهنشاه مالک رقاب　　بکشتي نه پیموده بحر آفتاب

1. *Pādshāh Nāmah* of 'Abdu'l-Ḥamīd Lahori, Vol. I, pt. I, p. 215.
2. *Ibid.*, p. 459.
3. *Ibid.*, p. 464.
4. This applies only to the Persians of the hinterland, for the Persians of the Gulf were expert mariners who sailed as far as China. See my *Persian Navigation*.
5. " His Majesty will put his foot on the tusks and mount the elephants." *Ā'īn*, I, p. 131.
6. Once she killed 4 tigers, two with one ball each and the other two with two bullets without missing. *Tuzuk*, p. 186 ; also *Ā'īn*, I, p. 525.
7. *Dīwān-i-Qudsī*, Bankipore MS., No. 684, f. 124^b.

Shāh Jahān's joy-ride on a white elephant in 1038 A.H. : " when he mounted the white elephant, the sun showed itself as it were over the white streaks of dawn " Kalīm) :[1]

بر فیل سپیدت که مبیناد گزند   شد شیفته هر کس که نگاهي افگند

چون شاه جهان بر او بر آمد گوئي   خورشید شد از سپیدهٔ صبح بلند

Prince Awrangzīb's cool courage during an Elephant Combat in 1042 A.H. when he was only 14 years of age : " when he found that his horse was unequal to the combat, he jumped on the ground and drew his sword : Afrāsiyāb would have melted with terror if at this age he had seen a raging elephant " (Kalīm) :

چو در اسپ سامان جولان ندید   چو شهبازي از خانهٔ زین پرید

هما ندم که بر خاک پا را فشرد   روان دست جرأت بشمشیر برد

درین سن اگر بودي افراسیاب   همي گشتي از دیدن فیل آب

Shāh Jahān's coronation in 1044 on the Peacock Throne " blazing like a lamp inextinguishable by water or any gust of wind " (Kalīm) :

توان ز آتش یاقوت آن چراغ افروخت   که نه ز باد رسد آفتش نه ز آب زوال

Shāh Jahān's conquest of the forts in the Deccan in 1045 : " he took in one year forty forts, not one of which could others have taken in forty years " (Kalīm) :[2]

چل قلعه بیک سال گرفتي که یکیش   شاهان نتوانند بچل سال گرفت

the lofty Dawlatābād fort " whose shadow has slapped the sky, blue in the face " (Qudsī) :

فلک را رخ از رفعت پایه اش   کبود است از سیلي سایه اش

the accident to Princess Jahān Ārā when her dress caught fire : " by contacting her dress, fire has acquired such dignity that angels may well make their rosaries of sparks " (Kalīm) :

تا کرده شعله کسب شرافت ز دامنت   زیبد اگر فرشته کند سبحه از شرار

and the gorgeous weighing-in ceremonies of Shāh Jahān " whose true equipoise could either be a mirror (so Mīr Yaḥyā) or his double (so Miān Mīr) put in the opposite pan : "

همسنگ تو در جهان نه بندد صورت   آئینه مگر نهند در میزانت

چیزي که برابري تواند کردن   در پلهٔ میزان تو عدل تو بود

are amongst the other interesting topics discussed by court-poets.

One duty of the court-poet, therefore, was to record social and political events. Another was to justify the abnormal acts of the King. When on the 5th Sha'bān, 987 A.H., Akbar alighted at the distance of ten miles from Ajmere and went on foot

1. *Padshāh Nāmah*, Vol. I, pt. I, p. 268.
2. *Ibid.*, Vol. I, pt. II, p. 181.

to the tomb of the saint Mu'īnu'd-Dīn Chishtī : " if the King goes on foot there is nothing undignified about it," said Fayḍī, " on the chessboard also the King moves on foot. "[1]

در عرصهٔ این جهان عجب نیست   گر شاه پیاده پا نهاده

رسمي ست که در بساط شطرنج   شه نیز رود ره پیاده

A third was to be with his sovereign through thick and thin, protect his honour and wash the dark stains on his character. How Fayḍī and Kalīm safeguarded the honour of Akbar and Shāh Jahān respectively are world-famous repartees but they do not lose their value by repetition.

An ambassador from Īrān came to Akbar's court, presented his credentials, and then read out in open darbār the following quatrain sent by Shāh 'Abbās the Great of Persia :

زنگي بسپاه و خیل و لشکر نازد   رومي بسنان و تیغ و خنجر نازد

اکبر بخزینهٔ پر از زر نازد   عباس بذوالفقار حیدر نازد

The Ethiopian is proud of his African guards ; the Turk, of his Turkish spears ;
Akbar, of his vaults full of gold ; but 'Abbās, of 'Alī's sword, Dhu'l-fiqār.

Akbar glanced at Fayḍī who replied extemporaneously :

> Elysium is proud of its waters of Lethe ; the sea, of its pearls ; the sky, of its stars ; 'Abbās, of 'Alī's sword, Dhu'l-fiqār ; but the two worlds are proud of their Akbar in ' Allāhu Akbar '.

فردوس بسلسبیل و کوثر نازد   دریا بگهر فلک باختر نازد

عباس بذوالفقار حیدر نازد   کونین بذات پاک اکبر نازد

The Sulṭān of Turkey reproached Shāh Jahān with arrogance in calling himself Shāh Jahān ' King of the world ' when he was only ' King of India.' Kalīm put the Emperor in good cheer by replying that since Hind (India) and Jahān (world) are, numerically, identical, the right of India's King to be called ' King of the world ' needed no additional argument :[2]

هند و جهان ز روي عدد هر دو چون یکي ست   شه را خطاب شاه جهاني مبرهن است

The most exacting duty of any courtier is to defend the indefensible. I have discovered two efforts of this kind, one by Fayḍī and the other a really brilliant Machiavellian achievement by Qudsī.

Applauding Akbar's worshipping of the sun, Fayḍī says : " Behold the equitable distribution of gifts by Fate ! Alexander had a mirror ; and Akbar has the sun. The former only saw himself in the mirror ; the latter sees God in the sun."

قسمت نگر که درخور هر جوهري عطاست   آئینه با سکندر و با اکبر آفتاب

او میکند معاینهٔ خود در آئینه   این میکند مشاهدهٔ حق در آفتاب

1. Fayḍī's *dīwān*, India Office MS., No. 3155, f. 279a.

2. *Kulliyāt-i-Kalīm*, Hyderabad State Library MS., No. 1225, f. 28a.

Qudsī's task, however, was far more arduous. When he began writing his *Ẓafar-Nāmah*, a history of Shāh Jahān's exploits in verse, which now exists only in two rare MSS. in the British Museum and the Bankipore Library, he was confronted with a dark blot on Shāh Jahān's character—the murder of five princes, namely two nephews, Bulāqī and Garshāsp, sons of Khusraw ; two cousins, Hūshang and Ṭahmūrath, sons of Dānyāl ; and one half-brother, Shahryār, son of Jahāngīr. Shāh Jahān may have begun his brilliant reign with a dark deed of violence ; but Qudsī was not prepared to make the hero of his *Ẓafar-Nāmah*, a villain. That the King can do no wrong everyone knew ; but it was reserved for Qudsī to demonstrate what Shāh Jahān himself did not know that the King had done no wrong.

He who knows virtue and vice, knows that intriguers ruin the country.	عیان است بر واقف خیر و شر که ویران شود ملک از رخنه گر
By distrust, the country is ruined ; 'tis best to pluck from the roots the sapling of mischief.	شود ملک ویران ز نا اعتماد ز بن کنده بهتر نهال فساد
The heads of political intriguers should be under the earth and the body-politic cleansed of all impurities.	سر مفسد ملک در خاک به ز اخلاط فاسد بدن پاک به
Not all that grows from the body has to be preserved : toe-nails and finger-nails have to be paired.	ز تن هرچه روید نباشد بجاي بود چیدني ناخن از دست و پاي
Will the tree of desire yield good fruit if it is not pruned of its superfluous boughs ?	نکو کي دهد میوه نخل مراد نبرند اگر شاخ و برگ زیاد
With a double-edged sword 'tis best to strike off that head which is the source of dynastic strife.	به تیغ دو سر آن سر افگنده به که در کار ملک افتد از وي گره
To-day the eaglet emerges from the egg ; and tomorrow it begins to prey.	چو شاهین زد امروز از بیضه سر کند رغبت صید روزي دگر
Bulāqī, Ṭahmūrath, Shahryār ; and with the three of them, Hūshang and Garshāsp	بلاقي و طهمورث و شهریار بان هرسه هوشنگ و گرشاسپ یار
Were at Lahore under the surveillance of Yamīnu'd-Dawlah.	بلاهور بودند هر پنج شان یمین دوله افگنده در رنج شان
And when Khidmat Parast Khān brought to Lahore the warrant for their execution,	که در قتل شان خان خدمت پرست درآمد بلاهور فرمان بدست
How that statesman executed the warrant—I know that you know. Why say what he did ?	در اجراي فرمان سگالنده مرد چه دانم که داني؟ چگویم چه کرد؟

'Tis obvious to every man of common sense that Kingship knows no kinship ;	بلي نيست پنهان ـ طبع سليم	كه در پادشاهي نشايد سهيم
And no thinker can ever accept a partner for God or the monarch.	بنزد خرد ور نباشد روا	شريک جهان چون شريک خدا
If thou dost admit that the King is the "Shadow of God on earth," it follows that the One God cannot cast two shadows.	چه گوئي تو شد پادشه ظل حي	نباشد يكي را دو سايه ز پي
The King's mind was relieved of anxiety (for the public weal) when the thicket was purged of its tiger-cubs.	شدش لوح خاطر ز انديشه پاک	كه از زادهٔ شير شد بيشه پاک

PATRONAGE OF COURT-POETRY

The evidence of the royal donors and their contemporary annalists all goes to show that Humāyūn, Akbar, Jahāngīr and Shāh Jahān were extremely liberal in their patronage of poetry. Some poets became commanders of 5000, like Ghaznawī d. 983 A.H., Zayn Khān d. 1010, Ja'far d. 1021, and Ulfatī d. 1022 ; others received jāgīrs like Ghazālī d. 980, Fayḍī d. 1004 and Ḥayātī died after 1024; others again received cash grants for isolated odes. For example, Akbar paid Rs. 2,000 to Ḥaydarī, d. 1002:[1] Rs. 5,000 to Kāhī d. 988 and Rs. 10,000 to Marwī d. *c.* 979. Jahāngīr paid Rs. 1,000 to Naẓīrī d. 1022, and Rs. 5,000 to Sa'īdā-i-Gīlānī in 1027. Shāh Jahān gave Rs. 5,000 to Sa'īdā in 1042,[2] Rs. 2,000 to Dānish in 1066,[3] and to the poet Qudsī d. 1056 he gave Rs. 2,000 in 1042,[4] Rs. 5,500 in 1045,[5] 100 gold mohurs in 1049[6] and Rs. 2,000 in 1054.[7] Similarly the poet Kalīm received from Shāh Jahān Rs. 5,500 in 1044,[8] Rs. 1,000 in 1049 and 200 gold mohurs[9] and again 200 gold mohurs[10] in 1055. But curiously though they praise the patron's liberality : for example, Fayḍī says that 'Abdu'r-Raḥīm Khān Khānān[11] paid the poets in advance, before listening to their odes :

داشت چون اعتماد بر شعرا   صله پيش از مديح گفتن داد

not a poet ever mentions what he actually received from his patron ; and even the poets who received titles and jāgīrs are always complaining that they were underpaid and undervalued.

1. *Muntakhab*, text III, p. 218.
2. *Pādshāh-Nāmah* of 'Abdu'l-Ḥamīd Lahori, Vol. I, pt. I, p. 493.
3. *Shāh Jahān-Nāmah* of Ṣāliḥ Kanbu, Vol. III, p. 209.
4. *Pādshāh-Nāmah*, Vol. I, pt. I, p. 444.
5. *Ibid.*, Vol. I, pt. II, p. 142.
6. *Ibid.*, Vol. II, p. 153.
7. *Ibid.*, Vol. II, p. 400.
8. *Pādshāh-Nāmah* of 'Abdu'l-Ḥamīd Lahori, Vol. I, pt. II, pp. 83-84.
9. *Ibid.*, Vol. II, p. 420.
10. *Ibid.*, Vol. II, p. 468.
11. For his liberality see p. 49, n. 2.

Mullā Nūru'd-Dīn Tar Khān held a jāgīr in Sind and received from Humāyūn the title of Tar Khān. This was a Mughal title which was hereditary for nine generations and carried with it extraordinary privileges. The poet says, however, that he had nothing but waste lands with his title of Khān and on becoming Tar Khān, since "tar" means " moist," what little moisture there was in those lands seemed to evaporate :[1]

I have a complaint to make before the wise and perfect king against the Tarkhānate.	ز ترخاني هم او را شکوۀ هست بنزد خسرو داناي کامل
For if 'tar,' 'moist,' be subtracted from the Tarkhānate, there remains but the dry khānate and the honorary Khān.	که غیر از خان خشکي مینماند ز ترخاني تري گردد چو زایل

Ḥydarī says that Akbar's donation of Rs. 2,000 is difficult to get and even more difficult not to get ;[2]

سیم و زر انعام کردي لیک از خازن مرا   هم گرفتن مشکل و هم ناگرفتن مشکل است

while Ghazālī, the poet-laureate complains in his unique *dīwān*, Br. Mus. MS. Add 25,023, f. 47[b] that he was better off when he was not in Akbar's service, for he has been deprived of half his jāgīr and the old horse in his stable is a liability.

O King since nearly three years it is the talk of every Turk and Persian,	پادشاها سه سال نزدیک است کین سخن ذکر ترک و تاجیک است
That Ghazālī has received encouragement and patronage from Akbar, champion of Islam.	که غزالي ز اکبر غازي یافت دلداري و سرافرازي
When the news reached my friends and relatives, greed drew them here.	شد خبر دوستان و خویشان را طمع این سو کشید ایشان را
Hitherto my condition was not bad ; but my present state has brought me humiliation.	پیش ازین بد نبود حالت من گشت این موجب خجالت من
Especially since the lofty dome of the sky has cut off my supply of water from above.	خاصه وقتي که گنبد والا آب ما را برید از بالا
Vexation has annexed the realm of my heart : one-half of my jāgīr has been reduced.	ملک دل غصه را مسلم شد نیمي از جایگیر من کم شد
Either good fortune has deserted me, or else some malicious fellow has been spreading a tale.	یا مرا چشم بخت شد خفته یا خبیثي حکایتي گفته

1. Badā'ūnī's *Muntakhab*, text, Vol. III, pp. 198-199.
2. *Ibid.*, p. 218.

Or the sportive sky has been playing a trick or the King has been trifling with me.	یا شهنشه بمن مطایبه کرد	یا زد این نقش چرخ عیش نورد
All I had in cash and kind is exhausted; my servant has become my master, your obedient servant has become a slave.	چا کرم خواجه گشت بنده غلام	نقد و جنسي که بود گشت تمام
An old woollen jacket is my (Kashmīrī) shawl; an earthenware jug is my Chinese bowl.	ظرف فغفوریم سفالي شد	در برم صوف کهنه شالي شد
I am left with a dilapidated pony which needs my careful nursing.	که بتیمار او گرفتارم	زآنچه ماند است اسپکي دارم
Call it not a horse; it is worse than an ass, for an ass is more swift of speed.	خرکي خود ازو دونده تر است	اسپ‌نامش‌منه که کم‌زخر است
Its back is bent like a bow and its protruding guts are the bow-strings.	رودهٔ او بر آن کمان زه رود	چون کمان شکسته پشت فرود
That bow can never be drawn: it throws the arrow before the archer's feet.	تیر را پیش پا فگنده بخاک	آن کمان هر دم از کشیدن پاک
That pony is always prostrating itself with humility; and (to avoid being outdone in manners by an animal) I have also to come down on my knees.	من هم از مردمي زده زانو	از تواضع بسجده آمد او
'Tis marvellous how without closing its lips, the horse kisses the earth.	بوسها داد بر زمین ادب	طرفه این کش بهم نیامده لب
Call it not a horse: it is a stable of grief and sorrow; a dry stick like the horse (knight) on a chessboard.	خشک چوبي چو اسپک شطرنج	نه که اسپي طویلهٔ غم و رنج
When Mānī (Manes) painted a lean horse, he drew his inspiration from that horse.	گشته او را بلاغري ثاني	اسپ لاغر که زد رقم ماني
A spider it is, imprisoned in the web of greed—grown old by worrying constantly over oats and straw.	در غم کاه و فکر جو شده پیر	عنکبوتي بتار حرص اسیر
Before the universe had emerged from non-existence, a floral rein had been flung on that pony's head.	او گل افسار داشت بر سر خویش	از عدم سر نکرده عالم پیش
The farrier of the sun had shod its shoe before it had put bells on the neck of the celestial horse.	که جلاجل نداشت خنگ سپهر	نعلش آن روز بست فارس مهر

It bears a hundred scars of grief—and also the branding-mark of King Bahrām Gūr (d. 438 A.D.).	گرچه صد داغ درد و غم دارد داغ بهرام گور هم دارد
Now and then I mount it with an effort—like a fly sitting on a running sore.	من بر اوگه گهي نشسته بزور چون مگس بر جراحت ناسور
It never moves its legs : even if it is killed, it will not stir under the whip.	هرگزش دست و پا نمي جنبد تو بکشش او ز جان نمي جنبد
If so, how can I be happy ? How can I bear the King company?	از چنین است چون توان آسود همرهٔ شاه چون توانم بود
O King, save me from that horse : give me one of thy special chargers—	پادشاها ازو خلاصم ده يکي از توسنان خاصم ده
Swift of foot, rushing like the North wind and the zephyr, over seas and mountains ;	بادسيري که از بحور و جبال بگذرد تيز چون صبا و شمال
So that in the royal cavalcade I may not lag behind any horseman.	تا توان در مواکب شاهي کرد با هر که هست همراهي
Since thou dost fulfil desires and unravel knots, pass orders also for the grant of a jāgīr.	چون توئي کام بخش و عقده کشاي حکم جاگير هم کرم فرماي

The complaints of Ḥaydārī and Ghazālī are innocuous ; but Sayyidī of Garmsīr passes beyond complaint to impugning the administration of Akbar, and having served him and various Amīrs, rejects, from his retreat in Kābul, the theory of Mughal liberality (*Muntakhab*, text, III, p. 247) :

Though in the reign of the king of the world, nobody possesses anything but a draught of water and a patched garment,	گرچه کس را بعهد شاه جهان جز دم آب و کهنه دلق نماند
Thanks a hundredfold to God, since poverty has become universal, there remains no envy among the people.	ليک صد شکر کز نهايت فقر حسدي در ميان خلق نماند

And again : " Thy generosity was not equivalent to my poetry : keep thy generosity and return my poetry."[1]

نه در برابر شعر من اين عطاي تو بود   عطاي خويش نگه دار و شعر من بفرست

The condemnation is singular but not unilateral : there are two rare instances of court-poets, namely Sanjar d. 1021[2] and Fanā'ī Chaghtā'ī, who were condemned and for a time even imprisoned by Akbar. Shāh Fanā'ī Chaghtā'ī became commander of 1000, served in the conquest of Mālwā and received the title of Khān but had later on

1. Badā'ūnī's *Muntakhabu't-Tawārīkh*, text, Vol. III, p. 248.
2. " For some crime, ' to mention which is not proper, ' Akbar imprisoned him. " See *Ā'īn*, I, p. 595, n. 3.

to be degraded. Once he said : " Nobody has excelled me in three shīns, shamshīr (sword), shī'r (poetry) and shaṭranj (chess)." Akbar at once replied : " the same might be said of two other shīns—shayṭānī (devilry) and shaṭṭāḥī (effrontery)."[1]

All poets, therefore, were not paragons of virtue ; and if occasionally, a poet was discontented with the Mughal court, Mughal patronage is not to be questioned, for though we know the King's liberality, the poet's rapacity we do not know. " The greedy fellow is like unto an oyster, " says Fayḍī, " which though drowned in a sea of water will nevertheless open its mouth to suck a single drop of water from the April shower."[2]

غرق دريا ست صدف ليک ز بسياري حرص   بهر يک قطرهٔ نيسان دهنش باز شود

When Bayram Khān had paid Hāshim of Qandahār, sixty thousand tankahs, equivalent to three thousand rupees, for a ghazal, " is this enough ? " asked Bayram. " Sixty is too little, " replied the greedy poet.[3]

---

1. *Muntakhab*, text, III, p. 296 ; also *Ā'īn*, I, p. 426.
2. *Dīwān-i-Fayḍī*, India Office MS., No. 3155, f. 281b.
3. *Muntakhab*, text, II, p. 36.

ODES FOR WHICH THE POETS WERE WEIGHED IN SILVER

ODES FOR WHICH THE POETS WERE WEIGHED IN SILVER

It is incredible what Indian enthusiasts can believe. Because the non-contemporary *Ma'āthiru'l-Umarā* must be right, Naẓīrī receives from Shiblī[1] what he never received from the Khān Khānān a lakh of rupees;[2] and because Akbar's *tankah* must mean a silver rupee, and Jahāngīr and Shāh Jahān's *zar* must mean gold, Naẓīrī, Ẓuhūrī, Ḥayātī, Sa'īdā, Kalīm and Qudsī receive from Professor Ghanī[3] what they never received from the Mughal Emperors or the rulers of the Deccan, their body-weight of gold, or elephant-loads of gold and silver, or 30,000 gold mohurs or even all the movable and immovable property of a Mughal aristocrat. Everyone knows, however, that non-contemporary works contain much ballast; and as for the *tankah*, my conclusion was reached much earlier by the *Khizānah-i-'Āmirah*, Neval Kishore edition, p. 390 :

> " The tankah is a double copper coin which is still in circulation : one rupee is equal to twenty tankahs; and therefore 200,000 tankahs are equal to Rs. 10,000."
>
> مراد از تنکه همین جفت پول مس باشد که بالفعل در زمان ما رائج است - یک روپیه به بیست تنکه میارزد - باین حساب دو لک تنکه ده هزار روپیه میشود -

And as for *zar* there are three passages in the contemporary *Pādshāh-Nāmah* of the court-annalist, 'Abdu'l-Ḥamīd Lahori which prove conclusively that zar was silver not gold : the word for gold being " zar-i-surkh : "

1. In 1042/1633 Sa'īdā-i-Gīlānī was weighed against zar and the value thereof amounting to Rs. 5,000 was given to him by order of Shāh Jahān (Vol. I, pt. I, p. 493) :

   سعیدای گیلانی ، مخاطب به بیدل خان ، این ماجرای مرد آزما در سلک نظم کشیده ، بعرض مقدس رسانید بامر خاقانی بزر سنجیده آمد و مبلغ همسنگش که پنج هزار روپیه بود باو انعام شد -

2. In 1044/March 1635 Abū Ṭālib Kalīm was weighed against zar and the value thereof amounting to Rs. 5,500 was given to him by order of Shāh Jahān (Vol. I, pt. II, pp. 83-84) :

   طالب کلیم ، چون قصیدهٔ رنگین بعرض اقدس رسانید ، بحکم شهنشاه دانش پرور بزر سنجیده آمد و بانعام مبلغ همسنگ که پنج هزار و پانصد روپیه بود کامیاب گشت -

---

1. *Sh'iru'l 'Ajam*, Vol. III, p. 143.

2. A list of 106 panegyrists and protégés of 'Abdu'r-Raḥīm Khān Khānān is given in the third volume of the *Ma'āthir-i-Raḥīmī* (Calcutta ed.) composed in 1025 A.H., which alleges that the Khān Khānān gave Rs. 10,000 and Rs. 12,000 to Naw'ī (p. 637) and Shakībī (p. 69) respectively for their *Sāqī-Nāmahs*; Rs. 12,000 to Anīsī on the occasion of his marriage in Lahore (p. 520) and a like amount to Maḥwī (p. 802), died 1016, and also to Taqīā'ī-Shushtarī (p. 681) who had expressed a desire to see what sort of a pile such a sum could make ; Rs. 50,000 to Ḥaydar Mu'ammā'ī (p. 622); Rs. 80,000 to Shakībī (p. 69), died 1023, for the journey to Mecca ; and to others, for example, 'Urfī (p. 297) such sums as beggar description. But before these figures are accepted, it should be remembered that " a great portion of the *Ma'āthir-i-Raḥīmī* is devoted to an ample detail of his patron, the Khān Khānān : it is written under such circumstances, in so fulsome a strain of eulogy, that it is difficult to know what faith to put in it." Sir H. Elliot. *History of India*, Vol. VI, p. 237.

3. *Humāyūn*, p. 150, footnote.

3. In 1045, the 16th of Shawwāl, Ḥājī Muḥammad Jān-i-Qudsī was weighed against zar and the value thereof amounting to Rs. 5,500 was given to him by order of Shāh Jāhān (Vol. I, pt. II, p. 142):

حاجي محمد جان قدسي را در جلدوي قصيدهٔ که بمدح پادشاه فلک پايگاه محلي ساخته بود بزر بر کشيده مبلغ وزن را که پنج هزار و پانصد روپيه شد باو مرحمت نمودند -

In those days one tola of gold was equal to Rs. 14 (*Pādshāh-Nāmah* of 'Abdu'l-Ḥamīd Lahori, Vol. I, pt. II, p. 79): "one hundred thousand tolas of gold, *i.e.*, 250,000 mithqāls are worth 14 hundred thousand rupees:"

يک لک توله طلا که دو صد و پنجاه هزار مثقال است و مبلغ چهار ده لک روپيه قيمت آن -

and if zar had been gold, the poets would have received fourteen times 5,000 or 5,500 rupees.

Obviously, therefore, when Jahāngīr says that he had Sa'īdā weighed against zar in 1027 A.H. (*Tuzuk-i-Jahāngīrī*, 'Alīgarh *ed.* p. 240):

بصلهٔ اين قصيده حکم فرمودم که سعيدا را بزر وزن کنند -

that zar was also silver. Furthermore, as Sa'īdā and Kalīm received Rs. 5,000 or Rs. 5,500 when they were actually weighed against silver, the poets Kāhī and Marwī who received from Akbar Rs. 5,000 and Rs. 10,000 respectively must be deemed to have been potentially weighed in silver. Finally, if material rewards are any indication of the quality of verse, then six super-poems of the Mughal period for which their composers were potentially or actually weighed against silver, should have come down to us. I shall now deal with those six neglected prize-poems of the Mughal period.

Writing only 14 years after Qāsim-i-Kāhī's death which took place in 988 A.H. the *Haft Iqlīm* says that for an ode in which the word 'fīl'—elephant—occurred in every couplet, Kāhī received one lakh of tankahs, *i.e.*, Rs. 5,000 (India Office MS., No. 49, f. 502[b]):

بواسطهٔ قصيدهٔ لازم فيلي که گفته بود يک لک تنکه صله گرفت -

Abu'l-Faḍl cites three verses of that poem but I have found the entire ode in the unique *dīwān* of Kāhī belonging to Prof. Mas'ūd Ḥasan Riḍwī of Lucknow:

Seeing that my beloved was interested in elephants, I have spent the cash of my life on the path of the elephant.	تا بفيلان ميل ديدم دلستان خويش را صرف راه فيل کردم نقد جان‌خويش را
On my head I throw dust like an elephant, wherever I go, if I do not see my elephant-driver on my head.	خاک بر سر ميکنم چون فيل هر جا ميرسم گر نه بينم بر سر خود فيلبان خويش را
So that my love may wax every moment, that elephant-driver drives his raging elephant very close to me.	دمبدم تا عشق من افزون شود آن فيلبان ميدواند بر سرم فيل دمان خويش را
I want to trumpet like a mad elephant all the time so that I may disclose my hidden secret.	همچو فيل مست ميخواهم خروشم هر زمان آشکارا تا کنم راز نهان خويش را

Rather 'tis better to hide love; 'tis best to bridle my tongue like an elephant.

بازميگويم حديث عشق پنهان خوشتر است
به که چون فيلان نگه دارم زبان خويش را

At the feet of the King's elephant (bishop), Qāsim-i-Kāhī laid his face (castle) and rolled up his chess-board of life.

قاسم کاهي بپاي فيل آن شه رخ نهاد
باخت آخر در بساطش خان و مان خويش را

The King who overthrows elephants is Jalālu'd-Dīn Muḥammad Akbar—he who bestows golden elephants on his poets.

شاه فيل افگن جلال الدين محمد اکبر است
آنکه بخشد فيل زرين شاعران خويش را

May the elephant of the sky be under the hook of his authority so that it may recognize its master, the Lord of Conjunction.

باد فيل چرخ زير چنگک فرمان او
تا شناسد خسرو صاحبقران خويش را

Induced by the reward given to Kāhī, the poet Ghazālī, d. 980 A.H., produced a poem contained in the unique copy of Ghazālī's *dīwān* in the British Museum, Add 25023 f. 50[a], wherein not only the elephant but also the hunting-leopard and lion occur in every hemistich:

Akbar, the champion, whose elephant, cheetah and lion are the elephant, cheetah and lion selected by the sky.

اکبر غازي که فيل و چيته و شير تو اند
چرخ ، فيل و چيته و شيري که کرداست انتخاب

I, Ghazālī, have written this poem in honour of thy elephant, cheetah and lion: to my elephant, cheetah and lion who can furnish a reply?

بهر فيل و چيته و شيرت غزالي گفت شعر
کيست فيل و چيته و شير مرا گويد جواب

But though Akbar was particularly fond of elephants and cheetahs and had made Ghazālī his first poet-laureate, the bloom of novelty had worn off and Ghazālī's *tour de force* evoked no material response.

The second prize-poem consists of 31 verses by Khwājah Ḥusayn Marwī, quoted in Vol. II, pp. 120-123 of Badā'ūnī's *Muntakhab*. "He received 200,000 tankahs *i.e.*, Rs. 10,000," says Badā'ūnī:

دو لک تنکهٔ نقد صله يافت -

All the first hemistichs of the ode give the date of Akbar's coronation, 963 A.H. and all the second hemistichs, the date of Jahāngīr's birth, 977 A.H. Sir Wolseley Haig says, footnote, p. 248, Vol. III, English translation of the *Muntakhab*, that 'this is not so;' and Mr. Lowe says, note 1, p. 127, Vol. II of the *Muntakhab* that the verses are correct, only sometimes a *waw* or a *ye* must be struck out. Actually, however, the ode contains 25 mistakes, vitiating 25 hemistichs. By collating with the 15 couplets contained in the *Akbar-Nāmah*, p. 348, Vol. II, Calcutta *ed.*, 1879, I was able to correct 8 mistakes; one mistake proved incorrigible and for the remaining 16 I have suggested emendations.

977 963

لله الحمد از پي جاه و جلال شهريار گوهر مجد از محيط عدل آمد در كنار

Praise be to God! For the sake of enhancing His Majesty's pomp and glory, a choice pearl has come ashore, from the ocean of justice.

طائري از آشيان جاه و جود آمد فرود كوكبي از اوج عز و نازگرديدآشكار

From the nest of rank and bounty, a bird has alighted; from the pinnacle of grandeur and elegance a star has appeared.

گلبني اينگونه ننمودند بر دور چمن لالهٔ زين گونه نكشود از ميان لاله‌زار

A rose like this was not displayed in the expanse of the garden: an anemone-bud like this did not blossom in the field of anemone.

دايهٔ ابر بهار از مهربانيهاي فضل 1673
سبزه با گل همزبان ، لولو بگوهر كرد يار 972
Read دايهٔ ابر بهار و مهربانيهاي رب 963
Read سبزه با گل همزبان ، لولو بگوهركرده يار 977

The wet-nurse of the vernal cloud and the blessings of God have made the verdure (Jodh Bai) a companion of the rose (Salīm), the pearl (Jodh Bai) an associate of the jewel (Salīm).

مهر ميگويد كه ميزيبد كه ،آن مه پاره را
از پي زيب جمال از زهره سازم گوشوار 979
Read از پي زى[1] جمال از زهره سازم گوشوار 977

The sun says: "to set off the beauty of that baby who is like a bit of the moon, it would be appropriate if I were to make an ear-ring of Venus."

مقدم مولود مي افزود زيب شه اگر لولوي لالا فزودي زيب درشاهوار

The welcome birth (of the Prince) has increased the splendour of the King, for now he has a lustrous pearl (Salīm) to match the royal pearl (Jodh Bai).

شاد شد دلها كه باز از آسمان عدل و داد
باز دنيا زنده شد كز مهر ايام بهار

All hearts are happy for once more from the heaven of justice and equity, the world has revived as if by the vernal sun.

آن هلال برج قدر و جود و جاه آمد برون
وآن نهال آرزوي جان شاه آمد ببار

Lo, the crescent hath come from the mansion of bounty, pomp and power: the sapling of the King's ardent soul has borne fruit.

شاه اقليم وفا ، سلطان ايوان صفا
شمع جمع بيدلان، كام دل اميدوار

The King of the realm of fidelity; the monarch of the palace of purity; the candle of the assembly of the broken-hearted; the desire of the hearts of the hopeful.

عادل كامل ، محمد اكبر صاحبقران
پادشاه نامدار كام جوي و كامگار

The just, the perfect Muḥammad Akbar, Lord of Conjunction; the illustrious monarch who pursues his desires successfully.

---

1. زى means form. See *Farhang-i-Anand Rāj*.

977 963

کامل داناي قابل ، اعدل شاهان بدهر عادل اعلي ، عاقل ، بي عديل روزگار

Perfect, wise, able, the most just king in the world; supremely tolerant, talented, the non-pareil.

از کلام او بیان حال معني مستفاد

وز کمال او بناي دين و دنيا استوار

From his speech is understood the meaning of the ecstatic state; by his perfection, the edifice of religion and the world is supported.

سايۀ لطف اله ، آن لايق تاج و نگين

بادشاه دين پناه آن عادل عالم مدار

The shadow of God's grace, worthy of the crown and seal; Defender of the Faith; the just pivot of the world.

بر زبان گاه از نجوم قهر آرد الامان 1028

Read بر زبان گاه از هجوم قهر آرد ای امان 963

با عدو گاه از زبان رمح گويد الفرار

With the onslaught of wrath sometimes he brings the word, "Quarter" on the tongue; sometimes by the tongue of the spear, he says, "Flee" to the enemy.

مجلس وي را سماء چارمين دان عود سوز

موكب وي را سماک رامح آمد نيزه‌دار

The fourth heaven is the censer of his assembly; the Arcturus, the lance-bearer of his cavalcade.

مركب منصور وي ز آنجا كه راند عالمي 1057

يمن گويد از يمين، يا يسر داند از يسار 877

Read موكب منصور وي ز آنجا كه راند ، عالمی 963

يمن گويند از يمين، يا يسر دانند از يسار 977

Wherever his victorious cavalcade passes, a world of people cry out: "Felicity" on the right hand, 'Prosperity' on the left.

حكم آن كلكي كه دارد حكم بر آب روان

بر سپيدي يا سياهي ميرود ليل و نهار

The power of his pen which exercises authority even over flowing waters makes (the record of man) black or white, night and day.

اي چو صنع لايزالي آفتاب ملک و دين

پايه افزاي معالي سايۀ پروردگار

Like the creative power of the Eternal God, O sun of the country and religion, thou makest eminence eminent and art the Shadow of God.

والي والا علم عالم دل و كيوان سرير

والی والا مآبي عادل عالي تبار 957

Read واليئ والا مآبي عادلی عالي تبار 977

O prince of the lofty standard, with a heart as large as the universe; Saturn-throned; thou art an exalted ruler, just and of noble descent.

مالک مال جهان اي پادشاه بحر و بر

با محبان مهرباني ، از كريمان يادگار

Lord of the wealth of the world; king of land and sea; thou art kind to friends (being a living) example of beneficence.

963 977

شاه صبح عدل و دادي ماه شام جاه و گاه   برق گاه عزم و جزمي كوه گاه بردبار

The sun of the dawn of truth and justice; the moon of the evening of pomp and dignity; (a flash of) lightning in taking decisions; a mountain in tolerance.

معدن عدلی و احسان ، منبع لطف و کرم 951
با بها و باذل و دین پرور و پرهیزگار 1697

Read معدن از عدلی ـ باحسان منبع از لطف وکرم 963
Read با بها و با دل و دین پرور پرهیزگار 977

Thou art a mine of justice; with benevolence, a fountain of grace and liberality; precious, magnanimous, chaste champion of religion.

حامي دين نبي اي ماحي آثار بد
والی والا علم ، کان کرم ، کوه وقار 894

Read والیئی عالی علم، کان کرم، کوه وقار 977

O protector of the Prophet's religion, O destroyer of evil traditions; thou art a ruler of lofty standard; a mine of bounty; a mountain in dignity.

نير برج وجودي ، گوهر درياي جود
از هواي اوج دلها شاه باز و جان شكار

Luminary of the mansion of existence; pearl of the sea of bounty; a royal hunting falcon soaring with an elevated heart!

كي بجودت ماند آبي از حيا پيش سحاب
با وجودت مي نزيبد جود از ابر بهار

At thy bounty, how can lustre remain to the blushing cloud? In thy presence, "bounty" is not applicable to the vernal cloud.

پادشاها سلک لولوي نفيس آورده ام
هديه كان آمد گرامي باز جوی و گوشدار

O king, I have brought a string of fine pearls: as the gift is precious, seek it and hear it.

کس نیارد هديهٔ زين به اگر دارد كسي
هر كه دارد گو بيا چيزی كه دارد گو بيار

None can bring a better gift than this: whoever has a better gift, tell him to come; tell him to bring the thing he has.

یک بیک اشعار مروي بسكه بي عيب آمده 1121
هر يكي جوئي ز وي مقصود دريابي دو بار 967

Read یک بیک ابیات مروي بسكه بي عيب آمده 963
Read هر يكي جوئي ز وي مقصودي دريابيدو بار 977

One by one the couplets of Marwī are so faultless that whichever verse thou triest thou wilt attain thy objective twice.

مصرع اول ز وي سال جلوس پادشاه   از دو يم مولود نور ديدهٔ عالم بر آر

The first hemistich thereof gives the date of the king's coronation; from the second, obtain the (date of) birth of the darling of the world.

تا بود باقي حساب روزهاي ماه سال
وآن حساب از سال و ماه و روز دوران پايدار

So long as the days of the months make up the year—and the day, month and year constitute the date,

شاه ما پاينده باد و باقي آن شاهزاده هم
روزهاي بيحساب وسالهاي بيشمار 976 ! sic

May our king and also the prince live—for countless days and innumerable years!

The last hemistich is short by one year. " A difference of one or two years, " says Abu'l-Faḍl, " is permissible in chronograms on buildings, not on persons' births and deaths. " However, Rs. 10,000 paid to Marwī induced the poet Ṣīrafī to produce a similar ode ; but it was too late : " the early bird had caught the worm, " says Badā'ūnī.

The third prize-poem is an ode by Sa'īdā-i-Gīlānī in honour of Jahāngīr and Prince Khurram Shāh Jahān. Only six verses quoted by Jahāngīr in the *Tuzuk* ('Alīgarh *ed.*, p. 240) have survived :

The nine heavens are an exemplar of thy threshold : aged Time hath become young in thy reign.	اي نه فلک نمونۀ از آستان تو　　دوران پیر گشته جوان در زمان تو
Like the sun, thy heart bestows largess without a cause : all lives are meant to be a sacrifice for thy gracious heart.	بخشد دل توفیض ونجوید سبب چومهر　　جانها همه فداي دل مهربان تو
Heaven is a green orange from the garden of thy power, suspended by thy gardener in the air.	از باغ قدرت است فلک یک ترنج سبز　　'نداخته بروي هو، باغبان تو
By God, of what substance art thou made, (O king), since from all eternity the souls of the saints have been deriving their lustre from thy sparkling life ?	یارب چه گوهري تو که افروخت در ازل　　جانهاي قدسیان همه از نور جان تو
O king of the age, may the world function according to thy desire—with thy Shāh Jahān flourishing (Khurram) under thy shadow.	بادا جهان بکام تو اي پادشاه عهد　　در سایۀ تو خرّم شاه جهان تو
O Shadow of God on earth, the world hath been illumined by thee, for thou art light (Nūr), and may the light of God always be thy canopy!	اي سایۀ خدا ز تو پرنور شد جهان　　بادا همیشه نور خد سایبان تو

Notice, in the concluding hemistichs, the double pun on Shāh Jahān's name which was Khurram, and Jahāngīr's name which was Nūru'd-Dīn. Jahāngīr was so pleased that he had Sa'īdā weighed in silver on the 14th Shahrīwar, 1027/26, August, 1618 : such an honour had never been conferred before and it was Sa'īdā's first performance !

In 1042/May, 1633 Sa'īdā beat the world's record when he was re-weighed against silver by order of Shāh Jahān for an ode depicting the cool courage of Prince Awrangzīb during an Elephant Combat. The Prince, less than 14 years of age, was charged by an infuriated elephant : he struck the animal on the forehead with his spear and when his horse was attacked, he leaped down from the saddle and again faced the animal. Just then aid arrived and the Prince was saved. Unfortunately not a single line of Sa'īdā's ode has survived : there are poets who do not receive honours but their works survive ; Sa'īdā received top-honours but his works have perished.

The fifth prize-poem is of 63 couplets by Kalīm on Shāh Jahān's second coronation on the Peacock Throne.[1] For this ode, Kalīm received Rs. 5,500. Rs. 5,500 for 63 verses, *i.e.*, 6 gold pieces per couplet ![2] And even so there are not six men in the world to-day who know that these 63 verses do exist. Why regret that the gems of the Mughal period are lost when this is our indifference to the gems that remain ?

Auspicious is the advent of New Year's day synchronizing with the Eid of Ramaḍān (first Shawwāl) : what flowers of joy have been showered on the (new) year and the (new) month !	خجسته مقدم نوروز و غرۀ شوال فشانده اند چه گلهاي عيش برمه‌وسال
At the festival of joy, there are two cups in the hands of the cup-bearer : aye, two crescent moons are necessary to enjoy the synchronism of the two Eids.	ببزم عيش دو جام است در كف ساقي ضرورت‌است‌بلي‌اين دوعيد را دوهلال
In the eyes of the people of the capital, a third Eid is the dust of the cavalcade of Shāh Jahān, who is a world of glory.	بچشم مردم دارالخلافه عيد نويست غبار موكب شاه جهان جهان جلال
Nawrūz receives 'exaltation' on such an Eid when the King takes his seat on the throne of absolute monarchy.	شرف پذيرد نوروز درچنين عيدي كه بادشاه نشيند بتخت استقلال
In praise of his throne, studded with gems, I am producing pearls of speech : God grant (him) Noah's length of life and continuity of speech (to me).	بوصف تخت مرصع گهر فشان گشتم خدا نصيب كند عمر نوح و طول‌مقال
Rubies from thousands of Ceylons and hundreds of Badakhshāns did the throne obtain as a gift ere it unveiled its beauty.	هزارسيلان ياقوت و صد بدخشان‌لعل برونماي گرفت است تا نموده جمال
The light of its rubies mingling with the lustre of diamonds is like the reflection of illuminations in crystal water.	فتاده پرتو ياقوت و لعل بر الماس چنانكه عكس چراغان فتد در آب زلال
Its antique emeralds are greener than fresh grass : who considers a combination of opposites impossible ?	زمرد كهنش تازه تر ز سبزۀ نو كه اجتماع نقيضين را شمرده محال ؟
The gold of the throne would have melted with the fire of its rubies—were it not for the water of its lustrous pearls !	طلاي‌تخت شدي آب از آتش ياقوت اگر نه قطره فشان ميشدي زلال لآل

1. *Kulliyāt-i-Kalīm*, Hyderabad State Library MS., No. 1225, f. 13^{a}-15^{a}.

2. Rs. 87 per couplet ; and as the value of gold then was Rs. 14 per tola, therefore six tolas of gold or six gold pieces per couplet.

With the fire of its rubies can be[1] lighted a lamp, inextinguishable by water or any gust of wind.	توان ز آتش یاقوت آن چراغ افروخت که نه ز باد رسد آفتش نه ز آب‌زوال
(The throne) hath no price but whatever else thou desirest it has: dignity, majesty, glory, grandeur, grace and beauty.	بها ندارد و دیگر هر آنچه خواهي هست ز شان و شوکت و فر و شکوه و حسن و جمال

There remains the sixth prize-poem of Qudsī which cannot be traced, being indistinguishably lost in his own *dīwān*. This is curious, because a poem for which the poet was weighed against silver should have stood out as a sapphire among pebbles. The *dīwān*, however, contains no such ode; and the conclusion is obvious: Qudsī was weighed against silver in 1045 for an earlier performance.

Shāh Jahān was a perfect artist who never had the same poet weighed twice against silver, nor two or more poets weighed against silver on the same occasion. Consequently, when Shāh Jahān took his seat on the Peacock Throne on the 12th March, 1635/1044 A.H. and all the three great poets of his court, Kalīm, Sa'īdā and Qudsī produced their masterpieces befitting that brilliant occasion, only Abū Ṭālib Kalīm was weighed against silver, not because he was the poet-laureate or because his performance was superior to that of his contemporaries, but because (*a*) Sa'īdā had already been weighed against silver in 1042 A.H., and (*b*) Ḥājī Muḥammad Jān-i-Qudsī, in so far as twenty of his verses had been inscribed inside the Peacock Throne, had, *ipso facto*, been suitably rewarded. Shāh Jahān felt, however, that Qudsī had not been materially compensated and so he was weighed against silver in 1045 for his performance of 1044. To proceed now to those verses which formed part of the Peacock Throne.

ENAMELLED VERSES OF THE PEACOCK THRONE

In 1037 A.H., shortly after his accession to the throne, Shāh Jahān selected jewels worth 86 lakhs of rupees and with them and a lakh of tolas of pure gold, worth 14 lakhs of rupees, he commanded Sa'īdā-i-Gīlānī to construct the Peacock Throne. Seven years later, in 1044 A.H., the throne was ready: it was 3¼ yards long, 2½ yards broad and 5 yards high, with two peacocks with upraised tails, carrying a ruby each in their beaks, on the quadrangular-shaped canopy of the throne. A jewelled tree separated the peacocks which faced each other; and 108 rubies and 116 emeralds, whose weight varied respectively from 100 to 200 carats and from 30 to 60 carats each, were studded on the outside of the throne. Twelve pillars of emerald surrounded with rows of round and lustrous pearls weighing 6 to 10 carats each, supported the throne; and three jewelled steps led up to the Emperor's seat whereon glittered a historical ruby worth a lakh of rupees, sent to Jahāngīr by Shāh 'Abbās the Great of Persia. And inside this throne, inscribed in enamel by order of Shāh Jahān, were the following twenty verses of Qudsī's (*Pādshāh-Nāmah* of 'Abdu'l-Ḥamīd Lahori, Vol. I, pt. II, pp. 80-81):

بامر خاقاني این مثنوي حاجي محمد جان قدسي که ختمش بر تاریخ است بمیناي سبز **درون تخت** کتابه نمودند-

---

1. Variant آب زلال.

Hail the auspicious throne of the King completed by the grace of God!	زهي فرخنده تخت پادشاهي	که شد سامان بتائيد الهي
For its construction, Heaven melted, first of all, the gold of the sun.	فلک روزي که ميکردش مکمل	زر خورشيد را بگداخت اول
By the Emperor's order, the blue of the sky went to the enamelling of the throne.	بحکم کارفرما صرف شد پاک	بميناکاريش ميناي افلاک
Of what use are jewels and gold save to embellish this throne ? For this purpose were the sea and the mine created.	جز اين تخت از زر وگوهر چه مقصود	وجود بحر وکان را حکمت اين بود
Its priceless rubies have made pale the ruby lips of sweethearts.	ز ياقوتش که در قيد بها نيست	لب لعل بتان را دل بجا نيست
To form its base, crown-jewels and the jeweller's art have been on the *qui vive* a whole lifetime.	براي پايه‌اش عمري کشيده	گهر افسر بسر خاتم بديده
To make this throne, the world was depleted of its gold, the earth, of its treasures.	بخرجش عالم از زر شد چنان پاک	که شد از گنج خالي کيسهٔ خاک
If the sky could reach the base of the throne, it would offer the sun and the moon as gifts.	رساند گر فلک خود را بپايش	دهد خورشيد و مه را رونمايش
The nobleman who rubs his head against the base of the throne is raised one step above the sky.	سرافرازي که سر بر پايه‌اش سود	ز گردون پايهٔ از تخت افزود
Its decoration is the tribute of the sea and mine : its shadow is (like) the shelter of the throne of God.	خراج بحر و کان پيرايهٔ او	پناه عرش و کرسي سايهٔ او
Glittering with multi-coloured gems, each one of which is a lantern to light the world.	ز انوع حواهر گشته الوان	چراغ عالمي هر دانهٔ آن
The floral gems of its panels shine like the light (of God) on Mt. Sinai.	در اطرافش بود گلهاي مينا	فروزان چون چراغ از طور سينا
Despairing of reaching the throne, Jams͟hīd has lent the gem (of his ring) to decorate the leg of the throne.	چو ميکرد از فرازش کوتهي دست	نگين خويش جم بر پايه‌اش بست
With the lustrous rubies and pearls (of the throne) the dark night can provide a hundred skies with stars.	شب تار از فروز لعل و گوهر	تواند صد فلک را داد اختر

Not because of its gems but because it kisses the feet of Shāh Jahān (when he takes his seat) has the value of the throne ascended to heaven.	دهد شاه جهان را بوسه بر پاي از آن شد پایهٔ قدرش فلک ساي
The world-bestowing King, full of youthful promise, spends all the wealth of the world on a single throne.	کند شاه جهان بخش جوان بخت خراج عالمي را خرج یک تخت
The God Who hath elevated the Empyrean, it is His Power which hath constructed the throne.	خداوندي که عرش وکرسي افراخت تواند قدرتش تختي چنین ساخت
Till the world exists, Shāh Jahān (King of the World) shall retain his seat on the throne.	اثر باقي ست تا کون و مکان را بود بر تخت جا شاه جهان را
A throne like this is his proper seat : the tribute of the Seven Climes lies at his feet.	بود تختي چنین هر روز جایش خراج هفت کشور زیر پایش
When the tongue wanted to express a chronogram, the mind suggested : *Awrang-i-Shāhinshāh-i-'ādil* (the throne of the just emperor).	چو تاریخش زبان پرسید از دل بگفت اورنگ شاهنشاه عادل

Which are better, the gems of the sea and mine or the gems of speech ? The gems *in* the Peacock Throne or the gems *on* the Peacock Throne ? Sa'īdā built the Peacock Throne but the following ode which he composed on that throne was finer. He could easily have been weighed a third time in silver or even in gold. It is a duty to Islamic culture to show that the most precious jewels of the Great Mughals were other than emeralds or diamonds.

THE UNIQUE ODE OF SA'ĪDĀ-I-GĪLĀNĪ

Sa'īdā's ode consisted of 134 couplets wherein each hemistich was a chronogram. The first 24 hemistichs (12 couplets) gave 1000 A.H., the date of Shāh Jahān's birth ; the succeeding 64 hemistichs (32 couplets) gave 1037 A.H., the date of Shāh Jahān's first coronation ; then followed a hemistich which gave 1043 A.H., the date of Shāh Jahān's return from Kashmīr for his second coronation ; and finally there were 179 hemistichs (89½ couplets) which gave 1044 A.H., the date of Shāh Jahān's second coronation on the Peacock Throne. Unfortunately, however, just as the Peacock Throne has perished and only some of its gems remain, so of the original ode, only 19[1] mutilated couplets survive in the *'Amal-i-Ṣāliḥ* or *Shāh Jahān-Nāmah* of Ṣāliḥ Kanbūh. Mr. Ghulām Yazdānī has edited this work in three volumes but not with the meticulous care of his later works, for the printed couplets, Vol. II, p. 90, contain

1. Actually 20 ; but I am disregarding one couplet which in all MSS. is so corrupt that it makes no sense.

all the errors to be found in MSS. plus errors of printing. Further, by offering no comment, the editor has perpetuated the blunder of Ṣāliḥ Kanbūh who states that the last 179 hemistichs give 1043 A.H. the date of Shāh Jahān's departure from Agra to Lahore en route to Kashmīr :

از هرمصرع نود بیت باقی تاریخ نهضت آن حضرت از دارالخلافه بسوي دارالسلطنت لاهور و نزهت آباد

کشمیر که عبارت است از هزارو چهل و سه معلوم میگردد -

Shāh Jahān was not going to Kashmīr : he was returning from Kashmīr in 1043 A.H. as the ode itself states : بسوئي هند ، عنان‌تاب زود شد با جاه : to take his seat on the Peacock Throne in 1044 A.H. And it was expressly to commemorate this second coronation that the ode was written : the last 90 couplets, therefore, give 1044 A.H.— with the exception of one remarkable hemistich which gives both in words and in number, the date of Shāh Jahān's return, *viz.*, 1043 :

هزار بود و چهل سه بسال از هجرت

Were all the errors of scribes and printers, author and editor, only to be reserved for the greatest poetical achievement of the Mughal period and one of the greatest achievements of the human mind ?

However I was confronted with 38 printed hemistichs whereof no less than 17 were incorrect. Eleven of these I corrected by collation with MSS. in the library of the late Nawwāb Sālār Jang of Hyderabad, and for the remaining six I am offering my own emendations :

Translation	Value	Hemistich
The One Incomparable God has caused the world to appear for the sake of Shāh Jahān, the King of the World.	1000	خداي واحد بیچون جهان نموده عیان
	1000	براي شاه جهان بادشاه کل جهان
By (his) justice, bounty and benevolence, the emperor of the globe : learned, exalted, patron of scholars and a conqueror.	1000	بداد و جود و باحسان شهنشهٔ آفاق
	1000	علیم و عالي و دانا نواز و ملک ستان
May he be king for a thousand[2] years, since he makes in the circuit of the globe, a hundred thousand lives happy !	741	هزار سال بماناد آنکه هر دم ازو
	1000	Read هزارساله[1] بماناد شه که هر دم ازو
	1000	بود بدور جهان صد هزارجان شادان
These twelve couplets in praise of Shāh Jahān has my mind, (co-operating) with my heart, produced on the tongue, by the decree of Fate.	1000	بمدح شاه جهان طبع این دوازده بیت
	1000	ز قسمت ازل آورد از دلم بزبان
Of those twelve, each hemistich, when written, is a chronogram of the birth of the King, the asylum of the world.	1000	از آن دوازده هر مصرعي بگاه نگار
	1000	کند تولد شاه جهان پناه بیان

---

1. For the use of ساله cf. Qāsim Arslān:

مبارک باد برصاحب قراني فتح بنگاله چنین ملکي سپاهش را میسر باد هرساله

2. In conformity with 1000 A.H., the date of Shāh Jahān's birth.

With a successful bid, he ascended the throne in Akbarābād, assisted by the all-knowing beneficent God.	باکبرآباد ، از جهد ، کامران بسریر **1037** جلوس کرد ز تائید عالم منان **1037**
It was in the year one thousand and forty-three of the Flight (1043 A.H.) when he came to Delhi with the (halo) of royalty and a mighty army.	هزار بود و چهل سه بسال از هجرت **1043** که شد بدهلي با شاهي و سپاه گران **1044**
In early spring there came to the garden of Sarhind, in his constant desire for a change of air,[1] the vernal flower (Shāh Jahān) smiling like the rose.	بنوبهار بیامد بگلشن سرهند **1044** گل بهارابد ، با هوا ، چوگل خندان **1044**
On the hills, are flowers of a thousand[2] hues ; and at every step of his, a thousand[3] streams, but better than the fountain of life.	هزارگونه بود گل بکوه و هر قدمش **1044** هزارچشمه ولي به ز چشمهٔ حیوان **1044**
Happy with the New Year and happy with the world, he decided to proceed (from Sarhind) to the city of Lahore.	ز کامراني نوروز عزم کرده نمود **1044** سوي مدینهٔ لاهور ، بر جهان شادان **1044**
Towards India he turned his reins quickly and went in all glory, driving like the blowing wind (his) dapple-grey steed swift as lightning.	بسوي هند عنان تاب **زد و شد** با جاه **1044** **Read** بسوي هند ، عنان‌تاب **زود شد**[4] با جاه جهانده برق نما ابرش چو باد وزان **1044**
With bounty and liberality, he returned to the capital : round his stirrups were the heavens ; and the angels round his reins.	بداد و جود بدارالخلافه آمده باز **1044** فلک بدور رکاب و ملک بدور عنان **1044**
A thousand thanks (to God) ! The beauty of the world has revived with the early glory of the throne of multi-coloured gems.	هزارشکر که بفزود باز حسن جهان **1044** ز نوبهار سریر جواهر الوان **1044**
On every land where from that (throne) a shadow fell, heaven bestowed till eternity the wealth and stock of a mine.	بهر **زمین** که از آن سایهٔ فتاده فلک **1094** **Read** بهر **زمی** که ازآن سایهٔ فتاده فلک **1044** بداد تا ابد دستگاه و مایهٔ کان **1044**
With the throne of the king of the times, beauty and lustre are displaying a hundred shades in the universe.	جمال و رنگ ز اورنگ بادشاه زمن **1044** **بداد گیتی** صد رنگ بر زمین و زمان **1228** **Read** بکار جلوهٔ صد رنگ بر زمین و زمان **1044**

1. The word هوا means both 'air' and 'desire ;' and I have tried to retain this double meaning in a free translation.

2 & 3. See note 2 on p. 60.

4. The error, here, is not numerical but عنان تاب as a compound word, followed by زود شد is better than عنان تاب‌زد و شد.

Lord from eternity, benefactor of all communities—he conquered the world sustained by the power of Faith.

خديو ملك ملك ، بادشاه دين و دول 1223
or خديو ملك و ملل بادشاه دين و دول 1239

Read خدا يگان ز ازل ، قبله گاه كل ملل 1044
جهان كشاد بامداد قوت ايمان 1044

O asylum of the world, O large-hearted emperor, thou art an ocean of generosity and of exquisite, infinite grandeur.

جهان پناها ، شاهنشهي و دريا دل 1044
محيطي از كرم و جود ليك بي پايان 500

Read محيطي از كرم و جاه خوب بي پايان 1044

With the terror of thy mace and spear, always does the heart of the enemy tremble underground, like a pulsating vein.

ز سهم گرز و سنانت دل عدو ، جاويد 1044
شود بزير زمين چون رگ جهنده طپان 1044

For this reason is thy foe's head like a black stone because it always provides a whetstone for thy spear!

از آن بود سر دشمن برنگ سنگ سياه 1203
كه از براي حسامت بود مدام فسان 1043

Read از آن بود سر دشمن بسان سنگ سياه 1044
كه از براي حسامت دهد مدام فسان 1044

The Arabs say that God in His mercy has given three things to three peoples—the hands to the Chinese, the brains to the Greeks and the tongue to the Arabs. But to the poet-artist Sa'īdā-i-Gīlānī He had given all the three—the Chinese hands, the Grecian intellect and the Arabian tongue.

POETRY OF MUGHAL ROYALTY

POETRY OF MUGHAL ROYALTY

THE poetry of kings is the king of poetry—this statement, though complimentary, is nevertheless true of the royal poetry of Mughal India, for Bābur and several of his descendants up to the fifth generation wrote and spoke poetry, even finer than the poetry of the poets they patronized. Unfortunately, however, though many are the admirers of Mughal culture in India, no one has attempted to sift the genuine verses of the Great Mughals ; and the *Cambridge History of India* does not even mention Humāyūn as a poet, though the unique *Dīwān-i-Humāyūn* which I have discovered in Patna fully corroborates the well-known fact that Humāyūn wrote excellent poetry. And the local scholars took no notice of this *dīwān*, thinking it was spurious, whereas it is genuinely the work of the Emperor and contains his pen-name in no less than eight verses :

Damsels of my adoration, seek from me neither sanity nor consciousness, for Humāyūn lies prostrate in an ecstasy of unconsciousness.	عقل و هو از من مجوئید اي بتان چون همایون بیهشي افتاده است
Verily in the condition of union with the Friend I had, like Humāyūn, unconsciously escaped from self.	حقا که چون همایون درحال وصل بیخود با دوست درحکایت از خویش رسته بودم
When Humāyūn looks at thy face (he says) : ' before me there is a veil of light ' (because excessive light is darkness).	همایون بروي تو چون بنگرد ' حجابیست از نور در پیش ما
O Humāyūn, as a legacy of love, a sigh is enough : the nett result of our love is air !	اي همایون ز عشق آهي بس حاصل عشق ما هوا باشد
Humāyūn, don't get restless because of her hair : the mischief of her amorous glances is enough for thee.	همایون ز مویش مشوش مشو ترا فتنهٔ غمزهایش بسند
I saw a Hindu lad in the rank of battle : rose-red was his face with the flush of wine.	هندو بچهٔ دیدم اندر صف جنگ رخسارهٔ او ز نشأمي گلرنگ

"I am distraught by thy wine-like ruby lips," said I. He parted his lips in smile. "Are these lips a stone, Humāyūn ?" he replied.	گفتم که خراب لعل میگون تو أم درخنده شد و گفت 'همایون لب وسنگ'
Humāyūn does not resent if he is denied the Supreme Paradise, for even Paradise is not worth the wandering of man (Adam) on earth.	نبودي جنت الماوا نبودي این همایون را که جنت هم بسرگرداني آدم نمي ارزد
I am nothing at all—devoid even of name : I am dependent on Thy grace, night and day.	من هیچ نیم هیچ نمیدارم نام بر فضل تو مانیم شب و روز مدام
Then for the sake of the Holy Lord of Lām (*i.e.*, the Prophet), shower upon this slave, Humāyūn, all Thy blessings.	آنگاه بحق حرمت مهتر لام بر بنده همایون برسان فیض تمام

Lām is the first letter of the Tradition : لو لاک لما خلقت الافلاک "if it were not for thee, I should not have created the heavens." The 'thee' refers to the Prophet ; so the Lord of Lām means the Prophet Muḥammad.

POETRY OF BĀBUR

The emperor, Bābur, had four sons, Humāyūn, Kāmrān, 'Askārī and Hindāl, born in 913, 919, 922 and 923 A.H. respectively, all of whom were poets : the last two are known by stray verses ; the first three by their *dīwāns*. Bābur's *dīwān* was published by Sir E. Denison Ross in 1910 ; Kāmrān's Persian *dīwān* of 186 verses, based on a copy stamped with the seals of the Mughal Emperors, has been published by the late Prof. Maḥfūẓu'l-Ḥaq of Calcutta ; and my edition of Humāyūn's *dīwān* is being published in the Silver Jubilee number of *Islamic Culture*. Bābur and Kāmrān were bilingual poets with this difference that Bābur wrote more in Turkish than in Persian, and Kāmrān more in Persian than in Turkish. Bābur quotes frequently from the great classical poets of Persia like Firdawsī, Niẓāmī, Sa'dī, Ḥāfiẓ and Jāmī ; and it is not always clear whether the verses given in the *Bābur-Nāmah* are Bābur's own compositions or quotations. For example, at the field of Panipat, Bābur recited the couplet :

پریشان جمعي و جمعي پریشان   گرفتار قومي و قومي عجائب

Mrs. Beveridge is not satisfied with her translation of this couplet because she could not trace it to its origin.[1] Professor Ghanī, however, has no such scruples : he traces it to Bābur himself as one of Bābur's spontaneous productions ;[2] though acutally,

1. *Bābur-Nāmah*, Vol. II, p. 470 : "A wandering band with mind awander : in the grip of a tribe (and) a tribe unfamiliar." "These two lines do not translate easily without the context of their original place of occurrence. I have not found their source," note Vol. II, p. 470.

2. *Persian Literature at the Mughal Court, Bābur*, p. 50 : "He (Bābur) recited off-hand a Persian verse which he compcsed on the spot."

9*

it is a quotation from an ode of the Persian poet, Salmān-i-Sāwajī :[1]

کنون پنج ماه است تا من اسیرم　　بغداد در در بلا و مصائب
پریشان جمعي و جمعي پریشان　　گرفتار قومي و قومي عجائب

It is now five months since I have been languishing in Baghdād in pain and misery.

Distracted by the mob, ruffled in mind : in the grip of a people and a strange people.

Bābur's citation, therefore, is very apposite : he finds himself distracted in mind, confronted with the vast and strange[2] Indian army. Mughal royalty produced good poetry because of a long period of apprenticeship under the great classical writers of Persia.

The genuine Persian verses of Bābur are only 19 whereof 13 are quoted here and six others, comprising 3 quatrains are to be found on pages 16 and 18 of the *Dīwān-i-Bābur Pādishāh* edited by Sir E. Denison Ross, Calcutta, 1910. The last quatrain, addressed to Mawlānā Riddle (Mu'ammā) was discovered by me in the Bankipore Library MS., *Bayāḍ*, No. 1998, f. 65[a] :

New Year and spring and wine and a sweetheart are good : Bābur have a good time for the world is not to be had a second time.

نو روز و نو بهار و مي و دلبري خوش است
بابر بعیش کوش که عالم دو باره نیست[3]

Spring has come but the lover who has no beloved takes no interest in the vernal air or the garden of tulips.

آمد بهار و دلشدهٔ را که یار نیست　　پرواي لاله زار و هواي بهار نیست[4]

I have seen much mischief upon the planet but not like the mischief in those eyes of thine.

در روزگار فتنه بسي دیده ام ولي　　چشم تو فتنه است که در روزگار نیست

Addressed to Niẓām Khān, Mīr of Bayānah, with a proverb in the last hemistich :

Strive not with the Turk, O Mīr of Bayānah : his courage and skill are obvious :

با ترک ستیزه مکن اي میر بیانه　　چالاکي و مردانگي ترک عیان است[5]

If thou comest not soon nor dost give ear to counsel, what need to explain what is patent ?

گر زود نیائي و نصیحت نه کني گوش
آن را که عیان است چه حاجت بیان است

Addressed to the late Khwājah Naṣīru'd-Dīn 'Ubaydullah, known as Khwājah Aḥrār, 806-895 A.H. :

We have wasted our life on the lower, the appetitive self and stand self-condemned before men of God.

در هواي نفس گمره عمر ضائع کرده ایم
پیش اهل الله از افعال خود شرمنده ایم

---

1. *Dīwān-ī-Salmān-i-Sāwajī*, p. 26, Bombay ed.
2. Tīmūr is said to have told his soldiers not to be afraid of the elephant for it merely carries its tail in front.
3. *Bayāḍ*, Bankipore MS., No. 1998, f. 64b.
4. *Ibid.*
5. *Bābur-Nāmah*, Vol. II, p. 529.

Cast a single glance on thy single-minded devotees for we have lived for the Master and are slaves of the Master.

یک نظر با مخلصان خسته دل فرما که ما
خواجگي را مانده ایم و خواجگي را بنده ایم[1]

The Khwājah's reply, projected from the grave :

Thy sincerity and faith have become manifest : thy condition and way of life have been proved (beyond doubt).

اخلاص و عقیدهٔ تو روشن‌شده است حالات و طریقه ات مبرهن شده است

Since there is no impediment in the way, arise and come quickly for thou shalt be looked after according to thy wishes.

حایل چو نماند زود بر خیز و بیا دلخواه تو تربیت معین شده است[2]

A chronogram on the conquest of Chanderī, 934 A.H. :

" Was for awhile the station Chanderī, pagan-full, the seat of hostile force.

بود چندي مقام چنديري پر ز کفار و دار حربي خرب

By fighting I vanquished its fort : *conquest of enemy country*, being the chronogram."

فتح کردم بحرب قلعهٔ آن گشت تاریخ : فتح دارالحرب[3]

Addressed to Mawlānā Riddle, Shihāb-i-Mu'ammā'ī :

Thy name has spread from Persia to Arabia ; and thy letter brings joy to the heart in pain.

نامت ز عجم رفته بملک عرب است وز نامهٔ تو در دل محزون طرب است

Always does the riddle lead to a name, but curiously, thy name leads to a Riddle !

هر کس بدر آرد ز معما نامي نام تو برآورده معما عجب است

Was Bābur thinking of the following couplets : " always the sea produces pearls but thy pearls (teeth) produce the sea (tears of the lover); " [4] " all men seek perfection but here is Perfection (Kamāl) seeking thee; " [5] " the Earth consumes man but I did not know that man consumed earth (the corn presented to the poet being full of sawdust),"[6] when he wrote to Mawlānā Riddle : "always does the riddle lead to a name but thy name leads to a Riddle ?" This rare poetical device is also found in the *Dīwān-i-Humāyūn* when entering Persia as a refugee, Humāyūn wrote to Shāh Ṭahmāsp : " all kings seek the shadow of the phœnix (humā), but here is Humā (Humāyūn) seeking the shadow of a king " :

شاهان همه سایهٔ هما میخواهند بنگر که هما آمده در سایهٔ تو

---

1. *Dīwān-i-Bābur Pādishāh, ed.* Sir E. Denison Ross, p. 16.
2. *Ibid.*, p. 22.
3. *Bābur-Nāmah*, Vol. II, p. 596.
4. Siḥāb-i-Iṣfahānī : صدف پروردن از دریا عجب نیست صدف بنگر که دریا پرورستي
5. Kamālu'd-Dīn-i-Iṣfahānī : جویان کمال اند بجان اهل هنر وآنگاه بجان کمال جویندهٔ تست
6. *Ibid* : خاک مردم خورد ندانستم که خورد مردم اي برادر خاک

to which the Shāh replied, quoting from Ḥāfiẓ:

His Majesty the Phœnix will fall into our snare
Should Humāyūn arrive with his stately air.

هماي اوج سعادت بدام ما افتد   اگر ترا گذري بر مقام ما افتد

Similarly, Shāh Jahān's poet-laureate, Kalīm, says of the water spouting from a fountain " always the sky rains water on the earth but here is the earth raining water on the sky : "

گر اول آمدي باران ز گردون   زمين بر آسمان ميبارد اكنون

POETRY OF HUMĀYŪN AND KĀMRĀN

My edition of Humāyūn's *dīwān* consists of 246 verses, comprising 16 ghazals, 60 quatrains, a mathnawī and fards ; but there is enough material embedded therein to interest not only the æsthete but the historian.

When Humāyūn ascended the throne in 937 A.H. he was advised to leave 'no rubs nor botches in the work,' but faithful to his father's dying injunctions, he spared the life of Kāmrān and received from him two congratulatory poems :

May thy realm perpetually increase ; may thy star continue to rise !	دولتت دمبدم افزون بادا طالعت فرخ و ميمون بادا
May the dust of thy road be the antimony for my eyes—dejected as I am !	هر غباري كه ز راهت خيزد كحل چشم من محزون بادا
May the dust which rises from the road traversed by the beloved (Laylā), settle in the eyes of the lover (Majnūn), its proper place !	خاک كو از ره ليلي خيزد جاي او ديدهٔ مجنون بادا
May a hundred Dariuses and Farīdūns be thy slaves, like me !	بندهٔ حلقه بگوش تو چو من صد چو دارا و فريدون بادا
Whosoever doth not encompass thee (with his love), may he be expelled from the vault of heaven !	هر كه گرد تو چو پركار نگشت او ازين دايره بيرون بادا
Kāmrān, as long as the world lasts, may Humāyūn be the king of the world !	كامران تا كه جهان راست بقا خسرو دهر همايون بادا

* * *

For several days our eyes have been on thy road, what if thou wert to take in our direction a step or two !	چشم بر راه تو داريم شد ايامي چند وقت آن شد كه نهي جانب ما گامي چند

He who never cares to send us a cup what if he were to regale us with his bad words, one or two!	آنکه هرگز نفرستد سوي ما جامي چند چه شود گر کنDم شاد بدشنامي چند
That others may not guess thou art my beloved, I pray for thy union with sweethearts, one or two.	تا کسي ميل دلم را برخت پي نبرد دولت وصل تو خواهم به دلارامي چند
To bait my heart, the grain of thy beauty-spot is enough: why lay snares with thy tresses, one or two?	بهر صيد دل ما دانهٔ خال تو بس است هردم از لطف منه بر سر ما دامي چند
Be not with us who frequent and haunt the tavern: alas that thou shouldst be in the company of libertines, one or two!	ما خراباتي رنديم تو با ما منشين حيف باشد که نشيني تو ببدنامي چند
Kāmrān, send this new lyric to Humāyūn: he may honour thee with gifts, one or two.	کامران اين غزل نو بهايون بفرست باشد ارسال کند سوي تو انعامي چند

For a time Humāyūn's cause prospered: he asked Bahādūr Shāh of Gujarāt to stop his aggressive campaign against the Rānā of Chitor, 941/1534:

O thou who art the enemy of Chitor, how (chaṭawr) shalt thou seize the infidels?	ي که هستي غنيم شهر چتور کافران را چطور ميگيري ؟
A king has come down upon thee: shalt thou seize Chitor sitting complacently?	بادشاهي رسيد بر سر تو تو نشسته چتور ميگيري!

But dark days were ahead: having lost the battles of Chaura, 1539 and Qanawj, 1540 A.D. and with them his brother's love, Humāyūn retreated to Lahore and wrote to Kāmrān:

Although one's image be seen in a mirror, it always remains apart from one's self.	در آئنه گرچه خود نمائي باشد پيوسته ز خويشتن جدائي باشد
It is strange to see one's self as some one else: this marvel is the work of God.	خود را بمثال غير ديدن عجب است اين بوالعجبي کار خدائي باشد

It is an extremely pretty quatrain: "being my brothe.," says Humāyūn," I thought you were my image, part of myself but like the image in the mirror which though part of one's self is apart from one's self, you remain apart from me and look upon me as somebody else: this unkindness on your part is by God's will."

Humāyūn did not lose heart: to his father-in-law he wrote in graceful verse:

He whose kernel is worth more than his shell, is our old friend, Bābā Dūst.	آنکه مغزش زياده است از پوست يار ديرين ماست بابا دوست

and with a few select friends, entered Persia as a refugee. His father had quoted Salmān-i-Sāwajī in his hour of trial: Humāyūn followed suit but with greater skill, so much so that it is perhaps the most apposite citation in all literature :

O king, the phœnix of my adventurous soul, hath since a long time made the summit of the Caucasus of contentment, its abode.

خسروا عمر يست تاعنقاي عالي همتم قلهٔ قاف قناعت را نشيمن كرده است

My enemy is Shīr (lion or Shīr Shāh) who many a time showed his back but has now turned his face towards me.

دشمنم شير است و عمري پشت بر من كرده بود
اين دم از راه عداوت روي بر من كرده است

I crave this favour of the king that he may do unto me what 'Alī did unto Salmān in the desert of Arzhan.

التماس اين ز شه دارم كه با من آن كند
آنچه با سلمان علي در دشت ارژن كرده است

There are four puns in this fragment : (*a*) the phœnix lives on Qāf, Mt. Caucasus, and qāf is also a letter of the Arabic alphabet, and the word قناعت 'contentment,' begins with this letter—so the phœnix (humā) lives on Mt. Qāf ; and the other phœnix (humā) Humāyūn lives in the Qāf of contentment ; (*b*) humā is the phœnix and also Humāyūn ; (*c*) one day in the desert of Arzhan, a lion confronted Salmān-i-Fārisī, Salmān the Persian, who called upon 'Alī for aid, and 'Alī appeared and drove away the lion—similarly will Humāyūn now be saved from his leonine adversary, Shīr Shāh, by Shāh Ṭahmāsp ; and (*d*) Salmān is both Salmān, the Persian, saved by 'Alī, and the poet Salmān-i-Sāwajī whom Humāyūn is quoting. In the works of Salmān-i-Sāwajī, the second couplet reads : طالعم شيراست *i.e.*, my horoscope is lion (Leo). Humāyūn changed it to دشمنم شيراست *i.e.*, my enemy is lion ; my enemy is Shīr Shāh ; and by altering a single word made Salmān-i-Sāwajī's fragment fit all the circumstances of his own case.

To the period of exile must also be ascribed the devotional verses which are the glory of Humāyūn's *dīwān*.

In praise of God:

O Thou Whose essence is everlasting, like unto Thee there is none : universal is Thy command ; pre-existence is Thy realm.

اي ذات تو لايزال مثل تو عدم امر تو على العموم ملک تو قدم

Even if the sea were ink, and the skies, the ink-pot, the pen would despair of describing Thy attributes.

گر بحر شود مداد و افلاک دوات عاجز شود از شرح صفات تو قلم

"Even if the sea were ink" is a quotation from the *Holy Qur'ān*, chapter 18, v. 109 : لو كان البحر مدادا .

In praise of the Prophet Muḥammad :

O Muḥammad, prince of the world in essential existence, verily thou art the friend of the living worshipped God.	حقا که توئي حبيب حي معبود	اي سرور کاينات در اصل وجود
Arise and display thy world-illuminating beauty, for thou art the purport of the world's creation.	زيرا که توئي ز خلق عالم مقصود	بر خيز نما جمال عالم آرا

* * *

Thou art the monarch of the throne of the prophets ; thou art the sun of the sphere of the saints.	خورشيد سپهر اوليائي تو	سلطان سرير انبيائي تو
Every one follows thy path : thou showest mankind the way of the Religious Law.	ره شرع بخلق رهنمائي تو	مردم همه پيروطريق تو اند

Having won Shāh Ṭahmāsp's favours by his graceful compliments :

The streaks of dawn flash forth from thy countenance : the gates of victory have been opened in thy face.	بر روي تو شد کشاده ابواب فتوح	اي از رخ تونموده انوار صبوح
For thee, my prayer to God is this : "Be ever happy ; unrivalled as a monarch ; like Noah in age."	در پادشهي فريد و در عمر چو نوح	خواهم ز خدا هميشه باشي خرم

Humāyūn took Kābul in 952 A.H.—he took Kābul کابل را گرفت, being the chronogram of conquest, 952. Then he wrote to his loyal governor, Bayram Khān of Qandahār (955 A.H.) :

Once again Victory hath appeared from the unseen world and jubilant are the hearts of my friends.	که دل دوستان ازو بکشود	باز فتحي ز غيب روي نمود
Thank God, once again we are happy—bubbling with laughter in the company of friends.	بر رخ يار و دوست خندانيم	شکر لله که باز شادانيم
Today is a sort of New Year's Day, O Bayram, when everyone is everywhere happy.	دل احباب بيغم است امروز	روز نوروز بيرم است امروز
Hereafter we shall think of India, and plan the reconquest of Sind.	عزم تسخير ملک سند کنيم	بعد ازين فکر کار هند کنيم

But Humāyūn had scotched the snake, not killed it: she closed and was herself again, that is, Kāmrān defeated Humāyūn in the field of Qipchāp and gloated in impromptu verse over the false news of Humāyūn's death :

A little breathing-time after the death of such an enemy I deem better far than a hundred years of life.

دمي حيات پس از مردن‌چنان دشمن　　گمان برم که ز صد سال زندگاني به

Humāyūn, however, regained Kābul, and Kāmrān fled to the court of Islām Shāh who treated him with scant courtesy. After telling the Afghan that the vicissitudes of fortune had imposed uncouth men over men of culture, Kāmrān sought shelter in Tattah where he was caught and blinded by order of Humāyūn. " Whatever thou metest out to me deserves my thanks, whether it be the blinding needle or the piercing blade " was the last and best poetical effort of this unfortunate prince.

Humāyūn was a mystic : " in movement the existence of the universe is like the water-wheel and the flow of water," says he apropos of this changing and yet unchanging world. And he had the mystic's premonition of his own impending death :

O God, with Thy infinite grace, make me wholly Thine : make me a gnostic of Thy Special Substances (Names and Attributes).

يا رب بكمال لطف خاصم گردان　　عارف بحقائق خواصم گردان

I am sore oppressed at heart by the tyranny of reason : call me Thy madman and release me from earthly bondage.

از عقل جفا کار دل‌افگار شدم　　ديوانۀ‌خودخوان وخلاصم گردان

This quatrain was produced spontaneously a few days before the fatal fall from the terrace in 963 A.H. " Humāyūn Bādshāh fell from the terrace : " همايون بادشاه از بام افتاد is the chronogram of death, but it is a wrong chronogram, short by a year.

POETRY OF AKBAR

Akbar cultivated his mind through the ear, not the eye—a remarkable instance of a person who did not know how to read and write and yet was steeped in culture. Here is an exchange of verses between Akbar and Khān Zamān of Jawnpūr who was eventually killed as a rebel in 974 A.H.

Khān Zamān's first quatrain :

Thy gate is the present times' Wall of Alexander : thy troops are Gog (and Magog).

اي سد سكندر زمانه در تو　　ياجوج بود سپاهي لشكر تو

Thy epoch reveals that the day of Resurrection has come, for thou art the Antichrist and Khwājah Amīnā is thy Ass.

در دور تو آثار قيامت پيدا　　دجال توئى، خواجه امينا خر تو

Khwājah Amīnu'd-Dīn Maḥmūd of Herāt was Akbar's bakhshī and commander of 1000 : he died in Nov., 1574 A.D. The other references are to the belief that just before Resurrection, Antichrist (Dajjāl) will come riding on his Ass and the tribes of Gog and Magog (Yājūj and Mājūj) will burst through the wall (Sadd) which keeps them back and will overrun the earth and eat up all the grass and herbs and drink up the rivers.

Akbar's reply :

O Khān Zamān, thy army is large, but my regime has given thee pomp and power.	شد دولت من باعث کر و فر تو	اي خان زمان که پر بود لشکر تو
May I be less than the Ass of Antichrist today, if tomorrow I do not cut off thy head.	فردا من اگر جدا نسازم سر تو	کمتر باشم ز خر دجال امروز

Khān Zamān's second quatrain :

Till there is a trace of crown lands in thy realm, hardly will thy troops fight me.	مشکل که بمن جنگ کند لشکر تو	تا هست اثر خالصه در کشور تو
Vaunt not thy gold and silver, for only thy servant will part with his head, for the sake of thy gold and silver.	از سرگذرد براي سیم و زر تو	بگذر ز زر و سیم که تا نوکر تو

Akbar's second reply :

Although the dust of my door is thy coronet, to-day thou dost not bow thy head before me.	امروز بمن فرو نیاید سر تو	با آنکه بود خاک درم افسر تو
From my good fortune accrues to thee gold and silver ; and that money has given thee thy military strength.	وز زور زر است ، قدرت لشکر تو	از دولت من هست ترا سیم و زري

Khān Zamān's third quatrain :

O King of the times, I am thy meanest servant, but fear deters me from approaching thee.	وز ترس نمي توانم آمد بر تو	اي شاه زمان منم کمین نوکر تو
From afar thou seekest my life, how then shall I seek thy shadow ?	نزدیک چسان توانم آمد بر تو	از دور تو قصد کشتن من داري

Akbar's final reply :

Since thou hast spoken the truth, may God befriend thee : may the blessings of God alight on thy parents !	صد رحمت حق بر پدر و مادر تو	گفتي تو چو راستي ، خدا یاور تو
Tamper not with my name on the coins and in the Friday sermons, so that I may not think of annexing thy territory.	تا من نکنم آرزوي کشور تو	تغییر مده تو سکه و خطبهٔ من

The contemporary *'Urafātu'l-'Āshiqīn*, Bankipore MS. No. 685 f. 222[a] does not state whether Akbar's replies were of his own composition; but the following three verses which the *'Urafāt* definitely ascribes to Akbar[1] were probably Fayḍī's, as suggested by Badā'ūnī (II, p. 268):

The Lord Who has given me the empire and a discriminating heart and a strong arm,	دل دانا و بازوي قوي داد	خداوندي که ما را خسروي داد
Has guided me in righteousness and justice—and has dispelled all other notions save justice from my mind,	بجز عدل از خیال ما برون کرد	بعدل و داد ما را رهنمون کرد
His praise surpasses man's understanding: Great is His Power; Allāhu Akbar!	تعالی شانه الله اکبر	بود وصفش ز فهم و عقل برتر

The last words, Allāhu Akbar mean both 'God is great' and 'Akbar is God,' wherefore, adds Badā'ūnī, "when Akbar read the verses on Friday the first Jumādī, 987 A.H., he stammered and stuttered." It is interesting to note that as the Emperor's name was Jalālu'd-Dīn Muḥammad Akbar, members of the Divine Faith used the ambiguous salutations: "Allāhu Akbar" and the reply, "Jalla Jalālahu."

Bābur and Humāyūn were fond of punning; so was Akbar. In Persian, kal is bald; and in Arabic, kalla is "not at all;" so apropos of the bald Yādgār Riḍwī who had revolted in Kashmīr, Akbar said: "Can the cap of sovereignty and the crown of royalty be acquired by a bald fellow (kal)? No (kalla), God forbid."

کلاه خسروي و تاج شاهي   بهرکل کي رسد حاشا وکلا

Similarly, "I don't take 'bang,' don't bring it: I don't play on the harp, don't bring it;" or conversely, "I don't take 'bang,' bring wine; I don't play on the harp, bring the lute"—for 'mayārīd' means 'don't bring' and 'may ārīd' means 'bring wine;' and 'nayārīd' means 'don't bring' and 'nay ārīd' means 'bring the lute.'

من چنگ نمي زنم ، نیارید   من بنگ نمي خورم ، میارید

or

من چنگ نمي زنم - ني آرید   من بنگ نمي خورم - مي آرید

Similarly, "I shall hide the secret of love from everybody: I am not mad or Majnūn to reveal it"—for in Persian literature, the lover par excellence is the mad Majnūn.

من سر عشق را ز همه کس نهان کنم [2]   دیوانه نیستم که چو مجنون عیان کنم

"If Salīm wished to be Emperor, he might have killed me and spared Abu'l-Faḍl," said Akbar, on hearing of Abu'l-Faḍl's assassination, and then recited the following verse:

My Shaykh was coming headlong to kiss my feet—and now he has come without head and feet.	شیخ ما از شوق بیحد چون سوي ما آمده [3] ز اشتیاق پایبوسي بي سرو پا آمده

1. f. 121[a]: این ابیات که خود گفته بود

2. *Bayāḍ*, Bankipore MS., No. 1998, f. 65*a*.

3. Blochmann, *Ā'īn*, Vol. I, Introduction, xxvii.

Similarly, the following verses of Akbar must have been produced spontaneously : the question of writing them out did not arise, the Emperor not knowing how to write :

In Majnūn's neck is not a chain to restrain his madness : Love hath put the arm of friendship round his neck.

نیست زنجیر جنون در گردن مجنون زار
عشق دست دوستي درگردنش افگنده است[1]

On the petals of the rose are not dew-drops but tears fallen from the eyes of the nightingale.

شبنم مگو که بر ورق گل فتاده است   کان قطره‌ها ز دیدهٔ بلبل فتاده است[2]

I shed tears of blood and emptied my heart : strange is thy love which makes me happy when I weep.

گریه کردم ز غمت موجب خوشحالي شد
ریختم خون دل از دیده ، دلم خالي شد [3]

Last night, in the lane of wine-sellers, I bought with gold, a bowl of wine.

دوشینه بکوي مي فروشان   پیمانهٔ مي بزر خریدم

And now I am heavy-headed with the after-effect : I gave gold to buy an aching head !

اکنون ز خمار سر گرانم   زر دادم و درد سر خریدم[4]

Bent is my back with the weight of sins, what shall I do ? Nor to the mosque nor to the temple leads the road, what shall I do ?

از بار گنه خمید پشتم ، چکنم ؟   نه راه بمسجد نه کنشتم ، چکنم ؟

My place is neither among pagans nor Muslims : unfit I am, both for hell and for heaven, what shall I do ?

نه در صف کافر نه مسلمان جایم   نه لایق دوزخ نه بهشتم ، چکنم ؟ [5]

POETRY OF JAHĀNGĪR

Among the virtues of the Great Mughals is a frank acknowledgment of vice : if Humāyūn was fond of opium : " I own treasures which are the envy of Crœsus, that is, I have opium in my purse : "

من گنج روان رشک قارون دارم   یعني که درون کیسه افیون دارم

Jahāngīr drank wine till there was a passage in his throat and drink in India : " drink wine to the garden in bloom : the clouds have gathered thick ; drink in excess : "

ساغر مي بر رخ گلزار میباید کشید   ابر بسیار است مي بسیار میباید کشید[6]

1. *Akbar-Nāmah.*
2. *'Urafātu'l-'Āshiqīn,* Bankipore MS., f. 121*b*.
3. *Ibid.*, f. 121^{b}.
4. *Ibid.*, f. 121^{b}.
5. *Ibid.*, f. 121^{a}.
6. *Tuzuk-i-Jahāngīrī*, Neval Kishore *ed.*, p. 235.

" We are ," says a fine Eastern satire," the reverse of Europeans : they are dynamic ; we are static. They write from left to right ; we from right to left. They consider wine lawful and drink in moderation ; we consider it unlawful and drink in excess."[1] Jahāngīr says that he composed the verse on the spur of the moment, and cites other examples of his impromptu verses : one of these was on a marble throne : " the seat of the King of the Seven Climes, Jahāngīr, son of Akbar, the King : "

نشيمن گاه شاه هفت كشور　　جهانگير ابن شاهنشاه اكبر

Another was on his own portrait sent to 'Ādil Khān :[2]

I look towards thee always with favour : sit securely under the shadow of my government.

اي سوي تو دايم نظر رحمت ما　　آسوده نشين بسايهٔ دولت ما

I am sending thee a portrait of myself : see then my inner self in the outer face.

سوي تو شبيه خويش كرديم روان　　تا معني ما بيني از صورت ما

and yet another was on the Jahāngīrī otto of roses sent to Khān 'Ālam when he was returning from Persia : [3]

I am sending thee my own scent to draw thee the more quickly to myself.

بسويت فر تاد ام بوي خويش　　كه آرم ترا زودتر سوي خويش

Like Bābur's memoirs, the *Tuzuk-i-Jahāngīrī* is full of quotations from the classical poets and gives specimens of the Emperor's own poetry.[4]

POETRY OF DĀRĀ SHUKŪH

Dārā Shukūh, the eldest son of Shāh Jahān, was not a dilettante : the *Sirr-i-Akbar* attests his knowledge of Hindu Philosophy : " in the Vedas and more especially in the Upanishads ," writes the Prince, " is contained the whole essence of pantheism. " In the realm of poetry his contribution is chiefly mystical quatrains which have been collected by Dr. Bikramajit Ḥasrat (see *Islamic Culture*, Vol. XVIII, pp. 145-164, 1944 A.D. where a reference is also made to an untraceable *dīwān* of 133 ghazals). Some good examples may be found in the *Ḥasanātu'l-'Ārifīn*, composed in 1062 A.H., where the Prince illustrates the pithy sayings of eminent mystics by verses of his own composition :

The gnostic will irradiate thy heart and soul : he will make a garden of the thorn plucked from his feet.

عارف دل وجان تو مزين سازد　　خاري كه كند ز پاش گلشن سازد

The perfect man will purge all defects away from every one : one burning candle will light a thousand candles.

كامل همه را ز نقص بيرون آرد　　يک شمع هزار شمع روشن سازد[5]

---

1. ايشان حلال ميشمارند وكم ميخورند ما حرام ميشماريم و بسيار ميخوريم

2. *Tuzuk-i-Jahāngīrī*, Neval Kishore *ed.*, p. 246. 3. *Ibid.*, p. 287. 4. *Ibid.*, p .77.

5. *Ḥasanātu'l-'Ārifīn*, MS. No. 553, Hyderabad State Library, f. 113a.

The gnostics are always in a new ecstatic state : they are religious leaders, not followers.	هر دم برسد بعارفان ذوق جدید خود مجتهد اند نه ز اهل تقلید
Lions eat only on what they have preyed : the fox eats the carcase abandoned in the sun.	شیران نخورند جز شکار خود را روباه خورد فتاده و لحم قدید[1]

* * *

Without death can thy name be immortal ? Without a servant can the master be noble ?	بي مرگ کجا نام تو گردد زنده بي بنده کجاست صاحبي زيبنده
'Tis the relative which manifests the Absolute : the master is master because of the servant.	از قید شود وجود مطلق ظاهر صاحب نبود اگر نباشد بنده[2]

* * *

Dost thou desire to be credited with insight ? Abandon, then, the wealthy state for the ecstatic.	حواهي که شوي داخل ارباب نظر از مال بحال بایدت کرد گذر
Thou becomest not a theist by saying : He is One ; the mouth is not sweetened by saying, 'How sweet !'	از گفتن توحید موحد نشوي شیرین نشود دهان ز نام شکر[3]

* * *

Was not the Father of mankind disowned by Satan ? Did not Ḥusayn (ibn-Manṣūr al-Ḥallāj) say, '(I am) the Truth,' and go to the gallows ?	ز ابلیس به بوالبشر چه انکار رسید حق گفت حسین و بر سر دار رسید
'Tis the evil and malicious spirit of the Mullās which has tortured every saint and prophet.[4]	از شومي و شر نفس ملایانست با هر نبي و ولي که آزار رسید

* * *

Death hath no sting for the mystic: the awakened heart fears no sleep.	از مرگ نباشد اهل دل را آزار وز خواب نترسد چو شود دل بیدار
If thy soul hath abandoned thy body, what matters ? When the skin becomes old, the snake casts it off.	گر جان تو جسم را بینداخت چه باک چون کهنه شود، پوست بیندازد مار[5]

" Paraded with insult through the bazaar of Delhi, the captive Dārā was murdered by some slaves of Awrangzīb (30th August, 1659) who had got the Mullās to issue a sentence that according to Islamic Law, Dārā deserved an apostate's death."[6] But the secular Republic of India will invest his name with a halo of glory and prescribe the verses which the Mullās had proscribed.

---

1. *Ḥasanātu'l-'Ārifīn*, Hyderabad State Library, MS. No. 685, f. 50*b*. 2. *Ibid.*, MS. No. 685, f. 50*b*-51*a*.
3. Cf. شیرین نشود دهان بحلوا گفتن which is a proverb. MS. No. 685, f. 44*a*. 4. MS. No. 685, f. 52*a*.
5. *Ḥasanātu'l-'Ārifīn*, Hyderabad State Library, MS. No. 553, f. 113*a*.
6. Sir Jadunath Sarkar, *Studies in Mughal India*, p. 41.

REPARTEES OF NŪR JAHĀN, MUMTĀZ MAḤAL AND ZĪBU'N-NISĀ

" Separate the living from the dead." In obedience to this law I have not mixed up the genuine verses of Mughal kings and princes, extracted from their own *dīwāns* or memoirs or contemporary works, with the verses of Mughal queens and princesses, whose authenticity has not been established. Sir Jadunath Sarkar does not accept the *Dīwān-i-Makhfī* as the work of Zību'n-Nisā ;[1] and the capping couplets here given may also be spurious, but they are too refined and elegant to be disregarded.

1. " I am not the nightingale, " said Jahāngīr, " to fill the air with my plaintive cries. I am the moth that dies without uttering a single moan : "

   بلبل نيم كه نعره كنم درد سر دهم   پروانه ام كه سوزم و دم بر نياورم

   " I am not the moth that dies an instantaneous death," replied Nūr Jahān, " I suffer a lingering death like the candle that burns through the night without uttering a single moan : "

   پروانه من نيم كه بيک شعله جان دهم   شمعم كه شب بسوزم ودم بر نياورم

2. " Thy collar, my love, has not been dyed with saffron, " said Jahāngīr, " engrained therein is the pallor of my face : "

   نيست جانان برگريبان تو رنگ زعفران   زردي رنگ رخ من شد گريبان گير تو

   " And it is the ruby-drops of my heart which have lent their hue to those ruby-buttons on thy silken coat, " answered Nūr Jahān :

   تراكه تكمهٔ لعل است بر لباس حرير   شد است قطرهٔ خون منت گريبان گير

3. " Why do old men go about with their backs bent ? " asked Jahāngīr. " They are seeking for their youth that is gone ," replied Nūr Jahān.

   چرا خم گشته ميگردند پيران جهان ديده؟(جهانگير)   بزيرخاک ميجويند ايام جواني را (نورجهان)

4. The task of awakening Shāh Jahān from his night's rest was entrusted to a maid-servant of Mumtāz Maḥal who, once misjudging the time, awoke the Emperor long before dawn. Thereupon Shāh Jahān lost his temper, came up to Mumtāz Maḥal and said : " The head must be chopped off " سر بريدن لازم است : " The head must be chopped off, " replied the Empress, " of that bird who hath sung before her time, for what does this fairy-creature know of dusk or dawn ? "

   سر بريدن لازم است آن مرغ بي هنگام را   اين پري پيكر چه داند وقت صبح و شام را

5. The lot of Mughal princesses was particularly unhappy for not being able to find eligible husbands, most of them had to remain unmarried. " O waterfall, " says Zību'n-Nisā, " for whose sake dost thou mourn ? For whose sake dost thou hang thy head in grief ? And what manner of pain was it that like me, through the life-long night, thou didst dash thy head against the rocks and weep ?"

   اي آبشار نوحه گر از بهر كيستي؟   سر در نگون فگنده ز اندوه چيستي ؟
   آيا چه درد بود كه چون ما تمام شب   سر بر زمين ميزدي و ميگريستي ؟

---

1. Sir Jadunath Sarkar, *Studies in Mughal India*, p. 80 ; see also Muqtadir, *Persian Catalogue*, Vol. III, pp. 250-251.

6. Seeing Zību'n-Nisā on the palace-roof, dressed in a green sārī, the poet and governor 'Āqil Khān said: " A form dressed in green appears under the blue vault of heaven." " Neither force nor gold nor guile will bring her to thee (by heaven), " replied Zību'n-Nisā.

سبز پوشي بلب بام نظر مي آيد (عاقل خان) نه بزاري نه بزوري نه بزر مي آيد (زيب النساء)

And when 'Āqil Khān continued to press his suit,[1] she quoted from Sa'dī: " why should the wise man ('Āqil) commit an act which brings repentance in its train ? "

چرا کاري کند عاقل که باز آيد پشياني ؟

7. Two more smart replies are ascribed to Zību'n-Nisā. " Rarely has a piebald pearl (half black, half white) been seen, " was a stiff hemistich to complete:

در ابلق کسي کم ديده موجود

" Unless it be the tears of a damsel with collyrium in her eyes, " replied Zību'n-Nisā:

مگر اشک بتان سرمه آلود

8. Because of their excessive neatness, people think these verses have been faked. But the fact is that in Mughal India, poetry was in the air; and even the servants in the palace could recite and improvize verses. " The Chinese mirror is broken and gone," said an attendant penitently:

از قضا آئينهٔ چيني شکست

" All's well: an object of vanity and self-seeing is gone, " replied Zību'n-Nisā:

خوب شد، اسباب خود بيني [2] شکست

---

1. Sir Jadunath Sarkar, *Studies in Mughal India*, pp. 85-86: " From the life-sketch of Āqil Khan we find that he was at the same place with Zeb-un-nissa first at Daulatabad in 1658 (some ten months), then at Lahor in 1663 for a week only, thenceforth with the imperial Court at Delhi and Agra till his resignation in April 1669, again with the Court during the Rajput wars of 1679 and 1680, and finally at Delhi from January 1681 to 1696. It was only during the first and last of these periods that he could have been tempted to court the Princess by the absence of her august father. "

2. The best use of خودبينى is by the Persian poet Kamāl of Khujand who says of a darwīsh with a cut nose: " since the poor wretch has no nose— بينى why chide him for not looking beyond his nose ?"

نشايد جرم خودبينى برو بست که آن بيچاره خود ، بينى ندارد